EVERLASTINGS
The Complete Book of Dried Flowers

Patricia Thorpe

Illustrations by
Anita Marci and Mary Close

COLLINS

A QUARTO BOOK

First published in 1985
by William Collins Sons & Co., Ltd
London • Glasgow • Sydney • Auckland • Johannesburg

EVERLASTINGS: The Complete Book of Dried Flowers
was produced and prepared by
Quarto Marketing Ltd.
15 West 26th Street
New York, N.Y. 10010

ISBN 0-00-411981-9

Editor: Karla Olson
Art Director: Richard Boddy
Designer: Mary Moriarty

Typeset by BPE Graphics, Inc.
Color separations by Hong Kong Scanner Craft Company Ltd.
Printed and bound in Hong Kong by Leefung-Asco Printers Ltd.

Dedication

**For my mother, Natalie Thorpe,
who started me in everlastings,
as in so many things**

Acknowledgments

THERE ARE MANY MORE PEOPLE THAN I CAN MENTION HERE WHO I would like to thank for their assistance on this project. However, the contributions of a few deserve special credit. The arrangements of silica-dried flowers are the work of Mrs. Henry Macy of Cold Spring Harbor, NY. She is a great artist, the foremost in this particular field and a woman most generous with her time and knowledge. Gail Peachin, of New York Ironweed in Charlotteville, NY, created the wonderful wreaths in this book—her great inventiveness and sensitivity to the material are evident, and her energy as a gardener is indefatigable. Her workroom and garden and my own were photographed by Richard Duncan, an old and very close friend. His beautiful photographs here say everything possible about his fine eye and technical expertise; beyond that, he is a wonderful person to work with. Robert Gray, who photographed Mrs. Macy's arrangements and workroom, also trekked around Manhattan to photograph some of my work— his considerable talent is equalled by his patience and endurance. David Cole, my typist and word processor, was an essential part of this book. Besides having a mind-reader's talent for figuring out my handwriting, he maintained an interest in and enthusiasm for the topic and information throughout the project that was gratifying. I must also thank Harold L. Stults, Jr., my husband, lawyer, and friend. It was his energetic encouragement that got me to take on this project and his ability to write a strong legal contract that enabled me to get something out of it.

Contents

Chapter One

Enjoying Flowers All Year Long

EVERY AUGUST OR SEPTEMBER, GARDENERS and flower lovers look at the glorious abundance available and think, "But what will I do in November?" This question has, for centuries, prompted the answer: dried flowers.

It is unfortunate that there is not a more poetic, inspired, or inspiring phrase to describe this wealth of material and the processes by which it is obtained. "Everlasting"—or *"immortelle"* as the French prettily express it—is a more attractive term, but it is usually only applied to a small group of flowers (of which the strawflower—helichrysm—is the most familiar example) with papery dry petals whose substance is not noticeably different whether they are dead or alive. But not all dried flowers are members of this group, and

there is not a good phrase that also encompasses the rich variety of pods, seed heads, branches, leaves, and lichens that all contribute to a finished "everlasting" arrangement.

The purpose of this book is, in part, to broaden the meaning of the word "everlasting" and to bring liveliness and interest to the dead term "dried flowers." We can find new subtlety of color and texture in working with dried flowers; arrangements of this material have a boldness and sculptural fascination very different from fresh flowers. Wild plant material that is evanescent or insignificant when fresh can add much when dried. This book will offer a broader view of the world of everlastings and will inspire new ideas and give new information about the entire world of plants and flowers and how we use them.

Zinnias, marigolds, dahlias, and delphinium—all the brilliant colors of summer shine, gloriously alive in mid-winter.

ROBERT GRAY

___Botanical Names___

BEFORE WE BEGIN EXAMINING THE EXCITING possibilities of dried flowers, you are encouraged to learn to use the botanical names of the plants. In this book, you will see the abundance of plant material available throughout the world for drying. However, if you use local, vernacular terminology, you will never know which plants you are looking at, using, growing, or buying in your area. As soon as you step outside the narrow neighborhood in which you live and grow things, people will speak another botanical language. Learning the Latin name of a plant and the family to which it belongs will enable you to go anywhere in the world and recognize related plants.

It is true that there are vast groups of plants that are seldom referred to specifically except by specialists: the grasses, sedges, and rushes are an example. In some cases, when referring to a large class of similiar plants like the mustards, there is little need to be specific. And it is also true that the local plant names have a wonderful folk poetry about them that is very attractive. But if you are serious about gardening or flower arranging, try to learn the proper names. Learning the families, too, can help the arranger to see subtle resemblances between related plants. In fact, everything you know about a plant will enable you to use it better. The Latin names, too, are often very descriptive, and sometimes poetic as well. Even though some plants are reclassified and the botanical names changed, there is greater uniformity and stability in this terminology than in the countless local names.

What Is an Everlasting?

IN CHAPTER FIVE, WE WILL DESCRIBE IN DETAIL MANY of the best flowers for drying, but we won't limit our definition of everlastings to just the groups of plants listed. You should begin to have a general idea of what kinds of material can be dried, and then you can experiment freely with whatever material is available to you.

First, it is important to determine how a specific type of flower dies. Does it drop its petals in a heap? Do the petals turn various unattractive shades of grey and brown, or look mildewed? Do the petals have a high water content, like gladiolus, and shrivel to nothing but inky blobs? These are some

characteristics of flowers that are *not* suitable for drying. They are not iron-clad rules, but they will save you from some of the more obvious failures. Flowers that shrivel but retain some of their color and original form are good bets; ones with stiff petals or colorful bracts are worth trying. Plants with interesting silvery foliage usually dry well. Often flowers with tight clumps of small blossoms retain their shape better than lush, loose, open-petal varieties. While letting a live flower die in an arrangement in water is not usually the best way to dry it, it's one way to learn a lot about some of the possibilities, as well as to eliminate some obvious losers. The same applies to watching flowers die and plants go to seed in the garden—you will get a sense of when to stop the process of decay and which plants have usable pods or seed heads.

Drying Year-Round

YOU SHOULD ALSO REALIZE THAT GOOD DRYING material is available all year round. Too often, dried flowers are thought of at the last minutes of the garden, in the late summer or fall. By this time you have already lost the chance to dry some of the best summer flowers, not to mention the surprising number of late-spring plants that can be used. There is also a great abundance of material besides flowers that can be picked late into the year, when many plants are forming seed pods and the late berries and vines are ripening their fruit. In fact, collecting all through the year will result in a much more interesting and surprising variety for the arranger.

Most beginners don't realize that narcissus and tulips—so seemingly evanescent—dry beautifully in desiccants. The lovely pulsatilla that blooms in the rock garden in April forms a wonderful whorled silky seed head that should be harvested in May. Many of the early iris and species tulips form large pods if allowed to seed, as do muscari and *Fritillaria meleagris*. There are innumerable species of allium to dry—most of them, starting with the familiar chives in the herb garden, bloom throughout May and June. Both the flowers and, later, the seed pods of these useful onions can be dried.

As you become skilled in the use of desiccants, the lavish assortment of early summer blooms will tempt you more and more to try drying them. If you become interested in this method of drying, it is essential to work at it all the time. It is possible to dry only a few flowers at once with this process, and it is important that the flowers used are utterly fresh and in perfect condition. Clearly, it is best to dry a few each day throughout the season, especially if you are experimenting with many different species.

Even the long winter months will not be a barren time for collectors. First of all, there are some plants that should be harvested in late November or early December. The great arched sprays of brilliant hips from the *Rosa multiflora* turn the best color late in fall; use them in holiday displays until January, then recycle them in dried arrangements.

Gather branches on winter walks—this is the time of year when you can see the individual character of each species of tree. Branches are invaluable as the frames for large-scale arrangements. Look for old fruit wood or conifer branches encrusted with lichens. All these have a place in the various styles of flower decoration, either fresh or dried. Branches with galls are fascinating, and those with bird's nests make delightful accents. Because of their obvious woodiness, branches hold up for a long time and can be reused often, either with fresh or dried flowers. If used first with fresh flowers, some branches may break dormancy and sprout leaves, but you can easily pinch these off. (If you want to keep pussy willow for dried arrangements, don't use it in water first since it will drop its catkins—let it dry thoroughly.)

As you can see, between growing, gathering, drying and—if there is ever time to get to it—arranging, the dried-flower enthusiast could be busy full-time, year-round.

Possibilities for Urbanites

IN LATER CHAPTERS WE WILL DISCUSS IN DETAIL HOW to grow your own flowers for drying and how to collect material in the wild. But what options does the urban flower arranger—someone with no garden, little space, and very possibly no vehicle for weekend collecting jaunts in the fields—have? Everlasting arrangements should not be the perquisite of only the suburbs; in fact, there are more possibilities for their use in the city. Urban offices are greatly enlivened by arrangements of flowers, and often fresh flowers are too expensive or too messy for a business to maintain all the time. The same is true of the public lobby of an apartment building and other interior spaces where live plants are not the answer. Dried flowers in these places are enjoyed and appreciated by people who have little contact with the world of nature.

The principal problem for urban arrangers is not obtaining material but storing it. One thing that will become clear when we discuss various methods of drying is that space—quite a bit of it—is required. At least one good-sized closet or cupboard will have to be given over for air-drying. Find one with good ventilation but, more important, make sure it is warm, dark and—above all—*dry*. After bunches of material are dry, they can be stored in long, covered boxes. If your home or apartment has high ceilings, the bunches can be hung on racks high above the living areas, but they must be wrapped in paper to keep out dust and damaging light until they are used. Drying with desiccants requires much less space—small boxes or tins can be slipped in any corner and the finished flowers stored in boxes.

The urban flower arranger has a much greater range of material available from florists than does the suburbanite. The increasing sophistication of both city florists and their patrons has resulted in a growth of available flowers in recent years. Advances in the technology of packaging and shipping have been enormous. Flowers from as far away as Hawaii, South America, Holland, South Africa, and Australia arrive daily in urban markets. Along with this great flood of exotics—which dominates the shops in winter—there is an increased supply of wild flowers and roadside weeds throughout the summer and fall.

All of this beauty is available to the city dweller. Many of the tempting exotics—the fabulous assortment of protea species, for example—are expensive. On the other hand, you only need one or two to capture attention in an arrangement. Also, learn which flowers can be used in fresh arrangements, then dried afterwards. Though not recommended for most flowers, some—like the allium or heather species—dry better while slowly absorbing water. Using flowers like these—as well as statice and gypsophila—will stretch your flower budget, since you can have fresh flowers when company comes to dinner, then recycle them later. Ornithagalum, which is dried with desiccants, lasts so long in water that you can enjoy it for weeks before you dry it.

In the summer, there are masses of garden flowers and wild material for sale in the city, and usually they are not expensive. It is important to learn how to tell which flowers are completely fresh. Look for signs—limp, decaying leaves or stems—that indicate a flower may be past its prime. Observe the centers of composite flowers like zinnias—they are best for drying before they have begun to produce pollen. Select celosia that has not yet begun producing its thousands of tiny shiny black seeds. Avoid any material that has been refrigerated for a long period—the petals and leaves become waterlogged and do not dry well.

Find a florist shop with a wide and interesting selection and develop a good business relationship with the owners. Let them know the kinds of flowers you are interested in. They will be able to order in-season specialties like fresh strawflowers or gomphrena, and will also be happy to let you know

as soon as a new everlasting has come in from South Africa or South America.

Be aware, too, of the possibilities with foliage. There are many varieties of palm leaves that dry well—either the very long sword types, like pandanus, or the palmate forms. Scotch broom provides tall, graceful outlines, or can be tied into tight curves which it will hold when dry. Shops sell it fresh throughout the year. Acacia foliage, too, is an asset to arrangers. All can be used in fresh arrangements, then recycled. Familiar florist staples like the leather-leaf fern and the flat fronds of western cedar can be pressed between layers of newspapers. And we could scarcely overlook the ubiquitous eucalyptus, available fresh, dried, or prepared with glycerine in endless variations of size and shape.

Besides this vast assortment which would make even the country gardener jealous, there is a surprising number of grasses and weeds available in even the most urban environments. Needless to say, you shouldn't molest public parks or planted areas. In the early summer, vacant lots spring up with several varieties of mustard seeds, and often Queen Anne's lace and the hated, invasive polygonum find a home there later in the season. Many of these weeds come up in sidewalk cracks or around the edges of buildings and parking lots; they can be picked by any passerby. Vacant lots are bulldozed periodically, and there is no reason you should not pick their flowers first.

Now you are beginning to get a sense of the rich variety of material available to even the most city-bound flower arranger. Much more can be found by those who have access to the countryside or can grow their own in whatever limited urban space they have at hand. Even a windowbox can provide a continuous supply of marigolds, zinnias, ageratum, and geraniums—keep cutting them and drying a few at a time in desiccants. The resources available to the enthusiast are limited not so much by situation as by imagination. You will see creative possibilities everywhere when you expand your ideas of what to look for, and where to find it.

Chapter Two

Growing Your Own

IF YOU HAVE A GARDEN—ALMOST ANY KIND of garden—you could be growing flowers you can dry. In fact, it is very likely that right now you are growing good drying materials but have never realized their potential. (The only real exception to this is the woodland garden—few plants that grow well in deep shade can be dried.) If you have no interest in or possibility of starting a garden, there is still much good drying material available to you either in the wild or from florists and suppliers. However, many people who become seriously interested in drying and arranging flowers sooner or later want to grow them themselves.

It is beyond the scope of this book to provide all the information needed by the beginning gardener. There are many books on the basics of gardening, and the library of any horticultural society is a good place to look for them. The information provided in this chapter is addressed to those who have broken ground at least once and planted something—anything—in it.

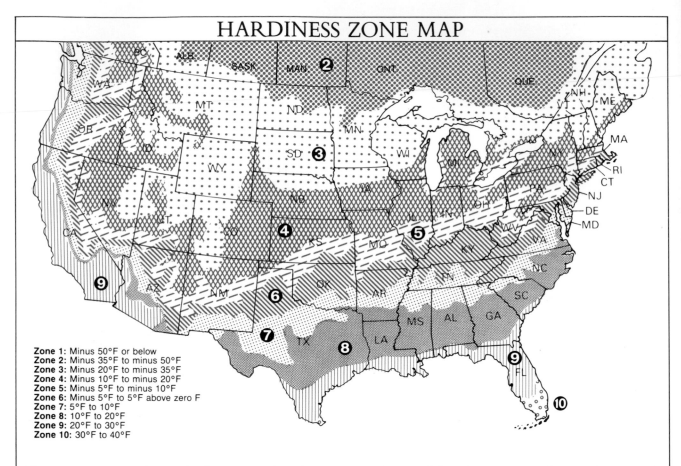

HARDINESS ZONE MAP

Zone 1: Minus 50°F or below
Zone 2: Minus 35°F to minus 50°F
Zone 3: Minus 20°F to minus 35°F
Zone 4: Minus 10°F to minus 20°F
Zone 5: Minus 5°F to minus 10°F
Zone 6: Minus 5°F to 5°F above zero F
Zone 7: 5°F to 10°F
Zone 8: 10°F to 20°F
Zone 9: 20°F to 30°F
Zone 10: 30°F to 40°F

There are two zones in the British Isles: Zone 9 along the western coastal areas of the Atlantic Ocean; and Zone 8 throughout the rest of the country. For a more specific assessment, simply match the average mid-January, noontime temperature range of your area to that of one of the zones listed. These instructions also hold true for Australia, though the mid-July temperatures should be evaluated. For both countries, convert Fahrenheit temperatures to Celsius by subtracting thirty-two from the °F, multiplying that sum by five, then dividing by nine: °C = 5/9(°F − 32).

Life Cycles

BEFORE YOU TRY TO GROW ANY PLANT, FIND OUT about its life cycle—or "habit of growth," as horticulturists call it. Does it grow, bloom, and die all in one year, or does it persist for generations, almost like a tree? Does it produce seeds or grow from a bulb? Does it disappear during the winter, or seem to stay alive year round? All of these considerations are important when deciding which plants to grow in your garden. Botanists and horticulturists have a whole dictionary of terms they use to describe each condition of a plant or the possible combinations. The array of plants that you can grow for drying is enormous; these considerations will help you decide which ones will work best for you and your garden.

Hardiness

HARDINESS IS AN IMPORTANT FACTOR CLOSELY TIED TO a plant's habit of growth. It is an assessment of a plant's resistance to certain environmental factors—mainly cold—which cause it to be long- or short-lived. The U.S. Department of Agriculture has divided the United States into numbered climate zones; these zone numbers are used widely, even outside of the U.S., to describe a plant's hardiness. In general, as defined in this book, a ''hardy'' plant is capable of surviving in the northern United States or Canada. Many factors besides climate determine whether a plant will survive a winter, but the hardiness zone numbers will help to reduce your chances of certain disaster when selecting plants.

The Basic Plant Categories

HARDINESS AND HABIT OF GROWTH COMBINE TO provide a kind of shorthand description of a plant and its ability to survive. Here are some descriptions of the types of plants you will find.

An *annual* germinates, grows, flowers, produces next year's seed, and dies all in one season. If a plant is a hardy annual, the seed can be planted outdoors early in the spring and the young seedlings will be able to withstand some cold spring weather. These plants will continue to flower through the summer if the blossoms are picked so the plant is not allowed to

go to seed. In the autumn, they will survive a mild frost and keep blooming until a really hard freeze. Examples of hardy annuals are alyssum, calendula, sweet pea, dill, and bachelor's buttons.

A half-hardy—or tender—annual has the same one-season habit of growth but cannot tolerate frost. Often these plants are of tropical origin and they frequently require a longer season of growth than is available in a northern climate. For the best results, the seeds should be started indoors and the plants set out after the danger of frost is over. (See more on Page 18.) They must also be brought in early in the autumn, as half-hardy annuals will turn black at the least touch of frost. Many of the best-known summer bedding annuals are tender, and often it is easier to buy flats or trays already half grown than to start them yourself. Some popular tender annuals are marigolds, zinnias, basil, and salvia.

A *biennial* germinates and grows for a season, is dormant during the winter, blooms the following spring or summer, then dies. Beginning gardeners may consider plants in this category a waste of time, since they have neither the quick satisfaction and long blooming period of annuals, nor the continuing yearly rewards of perennials. Nevertheless, this group of flowers provides some excellent drying plants and most will self-sow freely so that once the cycle has started new plants will bloom every year. Also, sometimes the biennial life cycle can be shortened by starting the seeds indoors early enough for the plants to bloom the first year. Seed catalogues usually call these ''quick-blooming'' biennials, but it will not work for all species. Well-known biennials are digitalis (foxglove), sweet william, lunaria (honesty or money-plant), and hesperis (sweet rocket).

Perennials usually bloom the second year from seed and may be expected to live for several years afterward. Some, like peonies, will outlive the original grower, while others seem almost like biennials. It is with perennials and biennials that hardiness becomes crucial. There is no point in trying to grow a plant that blooms the second year if

BULB PLANTING GUIDE

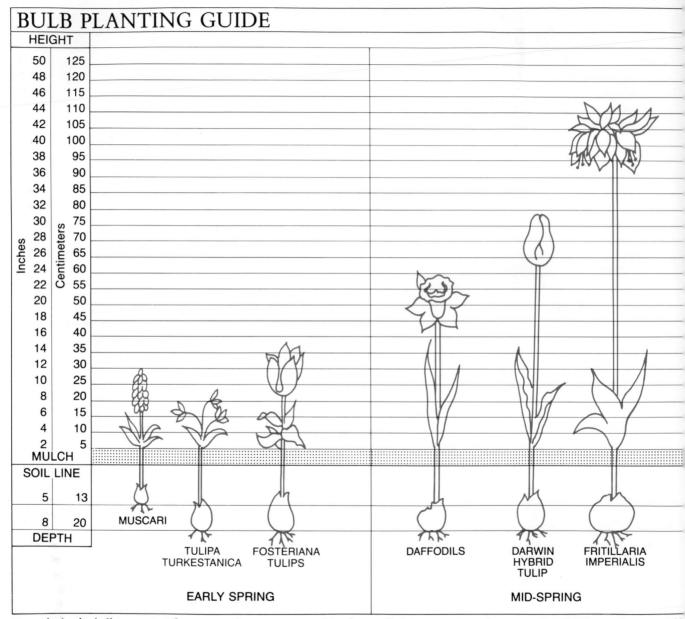

HEIGHT		
50	125	
48	120	
46	115	
44	110	
42	105	
40	100	
38	95	
36	90	
34	85	
32	80	
30	75	
28	70	
26	65	
24	60	
22	55	
20	50	
18	45	
16	40	
14	35	
12	30	
10	25	
8	20	
6	15	
4	10	
2	5	

Inches / Centimeters

MULCH

SOIL LINE

| 5 | 13 |
| 8 | 20 |

DEPTH

MUSCARI

TULIPA TURKESTANICA

FOSTERIANA TULIPS

DAFFODILS

DARWIN HYBRID TULIP

FRITILLARIA IMPERIALIS

EARLY SPRING

MID-SPRING

Versatile hardy bulbs are easy for any gardener to grow. This chart will help you plant them according to size and time of bl

16

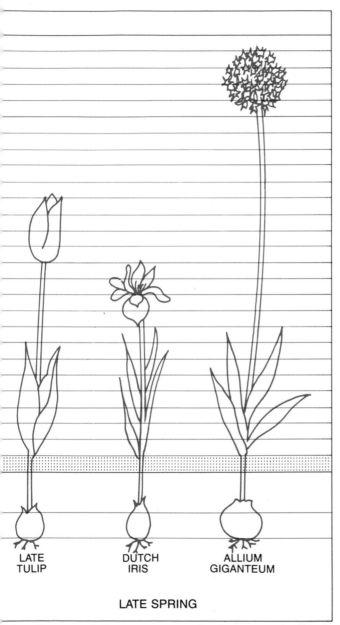

LATE
TULIP

DUTCH
IRIS

ALLIUM
GIGANTEUM

LATE SPRING

their flowers with desiccants, or wait for the interesting seedpods.

it won't survive the first winter. Some of these tender perennials can be cultivated as annuals if they are started early or grown in a cold frame. Fascinating as these tender plants are, growing them is much more confusing than rewarding, and beginners should ignore them. There are many, many hardy perennials for any climate zone and it is not necessary to search for the exotic. Some of the most familiar examples are peonies, artemesia, and baptisia.

Flowering bulbs are produced by an underground organ made up of scales of compressed leaves used for food storage. The hardy flowering bulbs are among the easiest and most rewarding plants to grow and include narcissus, tulips, lilies, and allium. Non-hardy bulbs, like the gladiolus, can be either grown as annuals, or dug up and stored at above freezing temperatures for the winter.

There are plants for drying in all these groups; it is up to the gardener to decide on the kind of plants and the amount of labor to be expended. A perennial garden is neither easier nor more difficult to cultivate than one composed of annuals—the kind of labor is different, as is the eventual effect.

Special Care for Annuals

IF YOU ARE A BEGINNING GARDENER OR ARE RENTING your property, you will probably want to grow annuals. Growing annual flowers is much like growing vegetables; in fact, a small section of a vegetable garden is a good place to begin growing flowers to dry. (There is probably even material from the vegetable garden that would be appropriate to dry!) Annuals in general require little soil preparation, and most of the good drying annuals are undemanding. Marigolds, zinnias, celosia, argeratum, gomphrena, annual salvia, annual statice are all annuals sold in flats or trays during the early spring; buying them this way will spare you the trouble of starting seeds yourself. Be sure to get the biggest double orange marigolds available; they shrink a great deal when dried. Have a variety of zinnias, but keep in mind that in this case the large double varieties are the most difficult to handle.

Larkspur (the annual delphiniums), the annual bachelor's buttons, *Centaurea cyaneus,* Iceland poppies, and nigella (love-in-a-mist) are all hardy annuals whose seeds can be sown very early in the spring—they need cold weather to germinate. Since these particular examples are difficult to transplant, be sure to sow them where you want them to grow.

The less well-known tender annuals will require a little more work for the gardener. The seeds must be germinated and the seedlings grown indoors from February or March until all danger of frost is over. Start the seeds in a shallow container of vermiculite or sterilized potting soil, or in individual Jiffy pots. Most of these seeds germinate best in a warm, dark place, and the soil must be kept moist. After germination, sunlight and air circulation are necessary to prevent fungus growth (damping off) and to insure good growth. Fertilizer that has been very diluted with water should be supplied. As seedlings grow, they should be transplanted into larger pots. During the indoor stages of growth, seedlings require good sunlight or special plant lights; before they are planted outside, the little plants should gradually be exposed to cooler temperatures (hardening off). Then, in late May, you are ready to start them in your garden. Helichrysum, xeranthemum, moluccella (bells of Ireland), amaranth are just a few of the tender annuals that can be started this way.

Once you have your plants in the garden, the rest of your summer gardening will be mostly weeding and watering when necessary. It is important to keep cutting off the flowers before they go to seed; most of these plants (the giant coxcomb celosia is an exception) will continue to bloom until frost if kept well cut. If you are continuously cutting flowers to dry, this should present no hardship.

Special Problems of Perennials

THE PREPARATION OF A PERENNIAL BED REQUIRES MORE work and planning than for an annual bed, since perennials are expected to live in one place for several years at least. A perennial garden must have deeper soil to accommodate long, large roots; the soil must be richer to provide greater nourishment year after year; and the drainage must be good, since heaving soil in the spring and standing water on the roots and crowns of the plants in the winter are both sure ways to kill most perennials. Also, many plants can withstand greater extremes of temperature if the drainage is good.

Once your bed is prepared, plants can be purchased already grown or you can start your own from seed. Seeds can be started right in the garden, or indoors as described for annuals. Perennials, in general, are slower to germinate and develop than annuals. This may be discouraging at first, but after the first year many of these plants become really large. During the first year, it is a better idea to disguise the bareness in the garden by filling the space around the perennials with annuals rather than planting young perennials too close together—you will have to move everything the next year when the plants are bigger and the space gets crowded.

One of the great pleasures of a perennial bed is arranging the plants in it. There are enormous varieties in size and shape between perennial species, which you do not find in annuals. Perennials bloom at specific times, some for a long period, some for a short period, some early, and some late. It is endlessly interesting to try to calculate which plants will bloom when, and how they will look next to each other. Once an annual bed starts blooming, it looks pretty much the same for two months, and then it's over. Perennial gardens look different every week and will offer many unexpected surprises and delights.

These masses of annual plants—the pink tufts of statice, the dramatically colored plumosa variety of celosia, and larkspur in a wide range of springtime shades—all dry easily and provide useful basic material for arranging.

Surprisingly enough, perennials, once they are established, are easier to grow than annuals. They are cheaper, too, because one plant can be divided in two or three years to produce many more plants. Dividing perennials may sound like another back-breaking job, and another reason to grow annuals. But remember, plants don't have to be divided every year; and when you divide them you will end up with loads of new plants to start new beds or to give to old friends.

Plants generally need dividing when the flowers get smaller and the roots become a tangled, choking mass. Some plants can be divided simply by cutting the root mass with a sharp trowel, shovel, or knife, keeping as much dirt attached to the roots as possible. Other perennials are more difficult to separate because their roots make an intricate series of knots that must be untangled slowly. In this case, it's hopeless trying to keep the dirt attached; it's best to slowly tease the roots apart under water, then replant them immediately. Root division should be done in the early spring or the late autumn. Plants with a single deep tap root, like *Asclepias tuberosa* and baptisia, should not be divided.

If you are diligent about picking the flowers of perennial plants, in some cases you will lengthen the period of bloom; in general, though, perennials have a shorter but more definite blaze of glory than annuals do. Generations of horticulturists have routinely recommended ''dead-heading''—cutting off finished flowers before they go to seed. For the gardener interested in dried flowers, there are disadvantages to this. Many perennials have beautiful seed pods that gardeners who cut back obsessively have never even seen. They argue that allowing the plant to seed diminishes its vigor. Considering the size and strength of most garden perennials, however, this is hard to take seriously. Allowing a plant to develop seed also gives it a chance to self-sow, and many plants grow much better from seed distributed in the natural cycle.

Self-sowing is especially important with biennials—once the cycle starts there will always be

Dahlias are among the best flowers for drying with s.

Select smaller varieties rather than huge cactus types.

ROBERT GRAY

blooming plants in the garden. The inexperienced gardener who attempts to sow the seed himself will often do it too early or too late. A garden that has sown itself has a wonderful flowing, natural look that cannot be achieved by scrupulous, but artificial, nurture. And, again, don't forget all those pods! Many gardeners are unaware that iris, lilies, and tulips all produce fascinating seed capsules that are beautiful in dried arrangements. So do many of the familiar garden plants. It is true that a garden with flowers going to seed will not have an immaculate, well-groomed look, but most of us have neither the energy nor the desire for that kind of perfection.

One reason that perennials are easier to grow than annuals is that once they are established, most species are more vigorous than all but the most tenacious weeds. The larger plants simply crowd out the competition. Also, since their roots are deeper and stronger than those of annuals, they need watering less frequently. Since many perennials can prosper for years almost without care, it is possible to grow a larger number of varied species than it is with annuals. Having fifty species of annuals in your garden would be a terrific amount of work, but a perennial garden of over a hundred kinds of plants could easily be cared for by weekend gardeners.

It is suggested in many books that the ideal garden is made up of both annuals and perennials. The idea is that space occupied by early blooming bulbs and biennials can be filled with late-blooming annuals like marigolds and zinnias. In actuality this doesn't really work, since most of the later perennials will crowd out the less-aggressive annuals. Annuals grow best in sections by themselves where the soil can be completely cleared and tilled each year.

As mentioned earlier, there are both hardy bulbs that grow like perennials and tender ones that can be used like annuals. Bulbs grow easily in any garden and mix well with other kinds of plants. Some bulbs will have to be lifted and divided periodically, but not as often as most plants. Many propagate both by producing seed and by making offset bulbs

The herb garden produces many possibilities for drying. Besides a wide range of flowers and pods, culinary herbs offer excellent fol

underground. Some species of lilies produce bulblets along the stem, which fall to the ground and plant themselves. Individual bulbs usually produce just one flowering stalk, but in time a clump will create a dramatic visual effect. And some bulbs—many of the allium species—are surprisingly cheap and practically foolproof to grow, even for beginners.

The Rock Garden

IN THE EVERLASTINGS CATALOGUE (SEE PAGE 47) YOU will notice some species of plants for the rock garden. It is, of course, not necessary to have a rock garden to grow flowers to dry, and the beginner

22

...terial and add lively aromas to arrangements and wreaths.

© RICHARD S. DUNCAN 1984

excellent. Species tulips and *Iris pumila* produce wonderful seed pods—enormous compared to the size of the plants. The petite *Delphinium chinensis* is one of the best subjects for drying with desiccants; many of the vast number of sedums dry well to produce good filler material. And there are many more possibilities.

The Vegetable Garden

THE VEGETABLE GARDEN WILL YIELD AN AMAZING array of materials for drying. Enormous plumes of rhubarb, beautiful leeks and white onions, gourds of fantastic shapes and textures, and fragile, airy stems of asparagus with brilliant berries are just a few of the possibilities. The leaves of ornamental cabbages and kales are lovely when dried. The herb garden also produces countless subjects for drying. The culinary herbs, for instance, in addition to their value in the kitchen, add lively aromas to wreaths and arrangements. The flowers of wild oregano, yarrow, and safflower are among the best everlastings; and parsley, dill, coriander, carroway, fennel, and lovage all produce tall umbels of seed that stay on the stem when picked and give a graceful outline to dried bouquets. In a water garden, Japanese and Siberian iris will flourish and make their pods; aruncus, astilbe, and filipendula will produce their frothy, feathery flowers and foliage.

As you can see from the many possibilities mentioned, everlastings are not just a narrow and specific segment of the plant world. In fact, no matter what kind of climate or growing conditions you have, no matter what garden scheme you want to develop, there are flowers you can grow and dry. And in spite of what sounds at first like a formidable amount of work, growing your own flowers to dry is enormously rewarding and, as you will discover, will provide you with a great deal of fun.

certainly does not have to start building screes and moraines in order to fill the drying cupboard. However, there are quite a number of alpine plants that make excellent dried material. Leontopodium—the edelweiss of many sentimental stories and songs—is one of the best everlastings, and armeria and the rock-garden varieties of yarrow are also

24

Chapter Three

Collecting
in the Wild

LET'S FACE IT: EVEN AN ENORMOUSLY PRO-
ductive gardener, growing all kinds of materials to dry, won't want, or be able, to grow
certain plants. But out along the roadsides
and hedgerows there is an abundance of wild
plants you can use. However, before you set
out to gather them, pay attention to this
cautionary conservation note.

The general public is much more sensitive
to conservation issues than it was years ago.
Many forces, including pollution, urban development, and highway construction, have
endangered certain specific environments
and, consequently, the animals and plants
they produce. But conservation awareness
must start with the individual, and it is
important to be constantly aware of the
delicate ecological balances needed to sustain
the life and beauty of the plants around us.

One result of this greater awareness in the
last 20 years or so has been the protection of
endangered species of plants. Lists of these
plants, specific to every country and often to
individual areas, are available, and none of
these plants should be picked or disturbed in
the wild. Although it is difficult to enforce
these rules, it is up to each individual to find
out what these plants are, and to respect the
regulations regarding them. There are also
certain particularly sensitive ecosystems with
such a fragile balance that they should be
avoided completely. Protected areas, natural
refuges, and parks should be respected so
that all can enjoy and learn from them.

Conservation bulletins and protection lists are available from any local park, cooperative extension, or national conservation agency. It is negligent to pretend not to know about endangered plants. The responsibility is yours, and if you are seriously interested in the beauty and delight flowers have to offer, you should be willing to do anything you can to protect them.

After this serious note, consider the cheerful fact that many of the best wild plants for drying are ranked as weeds and grow in the least threatened environments; most conservationists would applaud your ability to find beauty in what many consider weeds. This is why, first of all, it is important to be able to identify the plants we use as well as the ones we wish to avoid. There are certain commonsense rules to follow.

Guidelines for Gathering

FIRST, GET A GOOD FIELD GUIDE. THERE ARE MANY lavishly illustrated picture-book types, but most of these are not practical to carry when you go collecting. Get one that lists a wide range of materials, not just the pretty flowers. In America, the Agriculture Department Bulletin ''The Weeds of the United States'' is a useful source of information, since most of the species listed can be picked with impunity. Many guidebooks will mention if a plant is protected, or if it is regarded as an invasive alien. You can feel free to pick the latter.

Keep in mind these commonsense suggestions for protecting plants. Never pick a flower if you only see one or two plants in a large area (unless, of course, you know it is common in the area).

If you are gathering pods, wait until the seeds are ripe and ready to be dispersed. Shake them free from the pod and scatter them in the area where the plant is growing. In this way, the plant's life cycle will continue, and others will enjoy the plant.

© RICHARD S. DUNCAN 1984

Spectacular monarda is a protected American wildflower.

Always cut a stem cleanly; *never* pull a plant out by the roots. If you are cutting trees or large shrubs, use a strong lopper to avoid jagged, broken-off branches that are easily infected.

There are also some commonsense instructions for protecting yourself in the wild.

Wear sturdy clothing that covers your legs and arms. Good gloves are essential and should be worn during the entire excursion. Insect repellent and sunscreen are also important.

Use good equipment: top-quality secateurs are a very important tool, as is a medium-size lopper for branches. A small saw is optional. A sharp pocket knife is useful for stripping foliage and thorns, as well as for cutting string to tie the material in bundles. Newspaper can be used to wrap and protect delicate plants or seed heads until you get them home. It is also advisable to bring a deep bucket of water for flowers like rudbeckia and Queen Anne's lace that will be dried later with desiccants—they wilt very soon after picking but will revive if conditioned properly right away.

Learn to identify poisonous plants that you should avoid, for instance, poison oak, poison ivy, poison sumac, and stinging nettle. A run-in with any of these will ruin a day in the fields—and may have longer lasting negative effects.

Where to Go

NOW THAT YOU'VE ASSEMBLED YOUR EQUIPMENT, where do you go? Here, too, common sense should prevail.

Don't stop on a major highway, freeway, or busy country road. Narrow lanes, sharp curves, and bridges are also dangerous places to stop. You may cause a traffic hazard that should be avoided. Quiet back roads are best, but remember that plants on the margins of dirt roads will be covered with dust.

If possible, ask permission to pick in pastures or at the edges of cultivated fields. Most farmers will be delighted if you remove their thistles or goldenrod, but ask them first. It's also wise to inquire about any irate animals that may occupy pastures.

In more developed areas, annuals grow quickly in sites that have been cleared for building. These sites also offer some of the best weeds for drying.

Waste areas and dumps—unattractive as they may be in many ways—are good places to collect. Also, look at the edges of parking lots, behind shopping centers, and in drainage ditches for other types of vegetation.

The cool depths of a vast, mature forest are among the least likely places to find plants to dry. However pleasant it is to walk in these shady caverns, it is a waste of time from the point of view of the dried-flower collector. Some ferns can be picked to press (lay them flat between sheets of newspaper as you pick them), and you may want to try to preserve beech leaves with glycerine (put the stems in water until you get home). However, most of the beautiful woodland plants are extremely evanescent spring-blooming varieties. Besides not being good to dry, many more plants in this category are protected than are those among the field flowers. The edges of a wood are different, however. Here, hops and the twisting tendrils of the wild clematis clamber into the trees and the brilliant magenta of epilobium (fireweed) lights up the shade.

Any small stream, pond, or swamp offers a wealth of material to the collector. Sedges, rushes, and grasses abound, among them the huge cortaderia (pampas grass), and thypha, the ubiquitous cattail. *Myrica pensylvanica,* the strongly scented American bayberry, and baccharis, with luxuriant silver masses, are two shrubs you might want to gather here. Echinocystis, the spiny cucumber vine, frequently grows at the edge of streams, and *Iris pseudacorus,* with beautiful yellow blooms that become enormous hanging capsules, and *Iris missouriensis* may actually be growing in the water.

The area around the seashore has a precarious ecosystem that is probably best avoided. While the sand dunes and salt marshes have indigenous plants of tempting beauty—limonium, the lovely sea lavender, is a good example—many of these are protected. Often, an entire seaside area is part of a state park or wildlife trust and should be left untouched.

The Collecting Procedure

NOW THAT YOU HAVE SOME IDEAS ABOUT PLACES TO go—as well as those to avoid—here are some suggestions for a collecting procedure.

Go on a dry day. It is essential that the material you pick be as dry as possible from the start. The late afternoon is a preferable time to gather, after the heat of the day has passed, but before the evening damp has set in. It is especially important to avoid high midday temperatures if you are collecting material to dry with desiccants. Even if you put your specimens immediately into water, midday heat may wilt them irreparably before you get home.

It is easiest to pick a large quantity of one kind of material at a time. As you cut each stalk, strip the leaves from the stem immediately. When you have enough stems for a bunch, tie them together with string or a rubber band. Doing these preparations in the field has several advantages: the bulk of the plants to be transported will be reduced; much of the mess will be left in the field, where it will decay profitably; and it is much easier to work with fresh material than with leaves, stems, and flowers that have gone limp. For your own safety, immediately remove all thorns from stems.

Even material that won't have to be hung, like pods and grasses will be easier to handle and sort when you get home if it has been bunched in the field. Try to remove any insects as you gather—often shaking the bunches will get rid of them, but you may want to spray the plants with insecticide just to be sure.

Some collectors bring boxes of sand or borax with them into the field and preserve rudbeckia or Queen Anne's lace immediately after cutting. This procedure has certain advantages, but it is not absolutely necessary. Instead, put the plants in water—the flowers will usually droop somewhat after they are picked, even in water—and bring them home to dry. As soon as possible, cut their stems again and immediately put them in hot water. If left in a cool dark place, they should be revived in a few hours. When they are turgid, prepare them for drying. (See Chapter 4, "Drying Methods," page 31.)

It is important to emphasize once again that gathering is not just a late-summer pastime. You will find different material available almost year round—don't limit yourself to just familiar plants and seasons. Obviously, much more material is available at the end of the growing season, but there are also berries and branches to gather in December. Try to pick flowers at all different stages of their development, especially if you are just starting to work with everlastings. The only way to discover the best time to dry a particular plant is to experiment. For example, if you dry some grasses while they are green, and some while they are brown, you will have a broader range of color to choose from.

Collecting in the wild has other advantages besides the abundance of materials you can amass. You will be come much more aware of the secrets of the natural world around you: the interplay between environment and plant; how and why a certain plant grows where it does, and how it reproduces; the factors that determine the dominant plant types in each specific location. These biological patterns become very interesting to anyone who gathers weeds in the fields. For the flower arranger, seeing plants in their habitats provides invaluable insight into how a specific flower exists in nature and inspires ideas of how to use it in art. We become more sensitive to the fine details of life around us and to the broader natural landscape—about which we can never know too much.

Complete dark is not necessary to dry material without vivid color, such as the polyganum, baptisia, and centaurea pods shown here.

30

Chapter Four

Basic Drying Methods

THERE ARE VARIOUS METHODS OF DRYING ALL the material you have either gathered or grown. As you will discover when looking at the Everlastings Catalogue (see page 47), several methods may be used on one kind of plant; sometimes the choice between procedures is dictated by personal preference, sometimes by the desire for a specific effect. But remember that all of these techniques have developed from personal experimentation. It cannot be repeated often enough that every individual will discover variations, and will experience success and failure in different areas. Try every one and find which works best for you and your selection of material.

Here are a few general suggestions that apply no matter what material is being dried and which method is used.

Dry much more material than you think you will need—by nature, the finished product is delicate and perishable, and breakage is inevitable.

All material must be thoroughly dry when you start. Never collect on a wet day. Pick your material after the dew has dried and before the evening damp sets in.

Use the most perfect material you can find—inspect it for blemishes, discolorations, and insect damage. Imperfections are magnified in the dried product.

Harvest material at the right moment. This is the most difficult condition about which to generalize, since the right moment varies enormously among different kinds of plants. Advice for specific cases is given in the Everlastings Catalogue, but this knowledge is the result of endless experimentation.

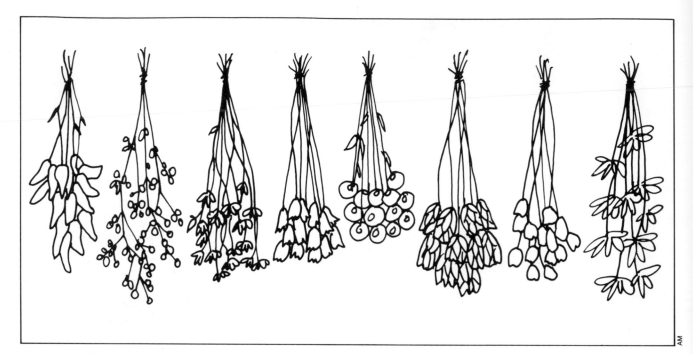

Air-Drying

"AIR-DRYING" IS A VERY GENERAL TERM THAT includes a number of different techniques with many variations. In the broadest sense, it refers to flowers dried naturally, without the use of any chemical desiccant. Most people envision thick bunches of drying flowers or herbs hanging upside down over the kitchen stove. However, the kitchen is, in fact, one of the worst places to dry or store material. What is needed is a warm, dark, dry, clean, well-ventilated space—like Grandma's attic.

Warmth, dryness, and good ventilation are essential conditions for air-drying because they all speed the drying process, and the best color and condition of the plants is achieved if they are dried as quickly as possible. The room where they are dried should be dark because sunlight damages all parts of a drying plant; it fades the color in the flowers, and breaks down the chlorophyll in culinary herbs, thereby destroying their flavor. Cleanliness is important because dust, soot, and grease adhere permanently to dried material, with lamentable results. The best conditions can usually be maintained in an attic, but if you have no attic, a large closet will suffice. It is easiest to keep everything hanging in the drying space until you want to use it; but if space is limited, the flowers can be removed and stored as soon as they are thoroughly dry, thus making space for new material.

It is best, although not absolutely necessary, to air-dry flowers as soon as possible after they are picked. In general, foliage does not dry well and should be removed immediately after harvesting, while the leaves are still fresh and easy to strip. (There are, of course, plants that you will want to dry specifically for their foliage; in that case, remove only soiled or damaged leaves.) After the leaves are stripped, gather the stems in a small bunch and

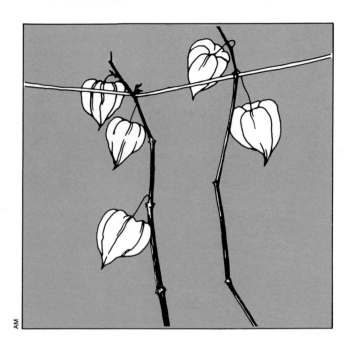

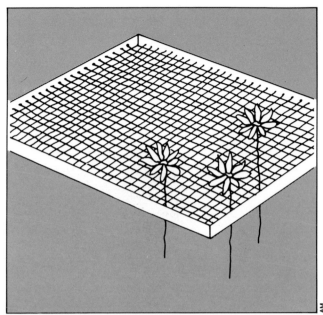

Here are some variations on air-drying—not all material should be hung upside down.
Hook physalis over a string so the lanterns hang the way they grow.
Wild carrot or leontopodium should dry face up. Place flowers on a screen with the stems hanging below; a cane chair is a handy alternative.
Maintain the natural curves of vines, such as clematis, by stretching them horizontally on a string.

The ultimate drying cupboard includes material hanging to air-dry, boxes of desiccant with flowers drying face-up, and silica-dried mat

...ed on wire screens, or with wire stems stuck in blocks of Styrofoam.

ROBERT GRAY

secure them with string or a rubber band—the stems will shrink as they dry, so make the string as tight as possible. The size of the bunch depends upon the kinds of flowers you are using, but usually 10 to 20 stems are enough; never make the bunch as large as a handful. It is most convenient to bunch only one species of flower, all roughly the same length. Avoid having all the heads press upon one another; that will hinder ventilation and distort the shapes.

Any kinds of racks, hooks, rods, or hangers can be set up to hold the bunches, as long as they are sturdy and accessible. A sheet of chicken wire hung under the ceiling will provide ample space for hanging. The bunches are usually hung upside down, which is more convenient because they will fan out from the narrow end of the bunch, and the weight of the flower heads will pull the stems straight while they dry. However, there are some cases in which this will not produce the desired effect: the bright orange Chinese lanterns of the physalis, for example, will dry opposite of their natural position if hung by the ends of their stems. They should be hooked individually over a string stretched horizontally. The flowers of *Daucus carota,* (the wild carrot or Queen Anne's lace) and leontopodium can be air-dried, but the petals of the flowers will curl closed if hung. Instead, they should be dried on a wire screen that has a wide-enough gauge to allow the stems to be inserted through, while it is still fine enough to support all the parts of the flower. The flowers will dry facing upward, with their stems hanging straight below. An easy (although somewhat eccentric-looking) variation on this is to dry them through the seat of a cane chair.

If all material is hung upside down to dry, the resulting arrangements will often look excessively stiff. Therefore, some material should be left to bend while it dries. For instance, grasses will assume more lifelike curves if simply stood upright in a container. Depending on the amount of space you have, they can also be spread flat on sheets of paper, but should be turned every few days at first to be sure they don't mildew or go flat on one side. Try to preserve the natural curves of vines like clematis or hops by looping them loosely over a string stretched horizontally.

Another variant of air-drying is called the "evaporation technique." In this method the flowers are allowed to stand upright in a container with their stems in an inch or two of water. The flower dries more slowly and in a more natural position. This method works especially well with allium, hydrangea, and heather.

Much of the late, non-flowering drying material—pods, berries, branches—need very little actual drying, but care should be taken to harvest them when their color and texture is best. Most of this material is less perishable than the flowering material and has little bright color to preserve. Masses of pods can be loosely bunched and stood upright in containers, or stored in large bundles or boxes. They don't need to be hung or stored in a completely dark place. Be sure they are completely dry first, of course.

The flowers of gomphrena and helichrysm—the familiar strawflower—air-dry easily; with odd, papery petals, their flowers seem dry even while they are still on the plant. But these need a little extra work to make them usable after they are dried. When the stems dry, they are not strong enough to support the large flower heads; as soon as the bunches are turned right-side up, the heads curve down into awkward, unattractive positions. So these flowers and others like them—xeranthemum, helipterum—should be wired before drying. Six- or eight-inch lengths of 21 gauge florist wire are most convenient—a false stem can be added later so they need not be longer. Snip the stem off ½ inch from the base of the head of the flower. Insert the wire up the stub of the stem and into the head of the flower. Take care not to push the wire too far in, or it will stick out the flower center—the center opens and shrinks while drying, so an obtrusive wire will ruin any naturalness of effect. The stem and tissues of the flower also shrink as they dry, fastening tightly around the wire—no gluing is necessary.

All of these techniques are methods of air-drying. In general, depending on where you dry them and how warm and dry your drying area is, most flowers and foliage will take three to five weeks to dry. Once dry, they can remain hanging until they are to be used. Most air-dried flowers are stable, though they will fade, especially if exposed to strong sunlight; and they will eventually become discolored by dust and dirt. Even though they are called "everlastings," these flowers are not meant to last forever and should be discarded and replaced, usually after a year.

Air-drying is the most widely used technique for drying. It is by far the easiest, and can be used for a very wide range of material. Even arrangers who utilize other, more difficult methods rely on air-drying for the bulk—the filler—for their arrangements.

Sand/Borax Method

IN SPITE OF THE EASE OF AIR-DRYING AND ITS effectiveness for many kinds of plants, there are some results it cannot achieve. When someone asks, "But can you air-dry a tulip to look like a tulip?" the answer has to be "no." But there are other techniques; many flowers can be dried to look life-like—it only requires patience, care, and the right technique.

Flowers have been dried with sand for many centuries—there is a detailed description of the technique in an early seventeenth-century Italian manuscript, and there is reason to believe that it was practiced much earlier. The only equipment this process requires is a large quantity of very fine, very clean, completely dry sand and a container. The sand must be without dust or silt; if very fine beach sand is used, it must be washed thoroughly to remove any trace of salt, then left to dry completely.

Flowers are placed in a container, then completely covered with the sand. The containers are left open to increase air circulation and evaporation. In this

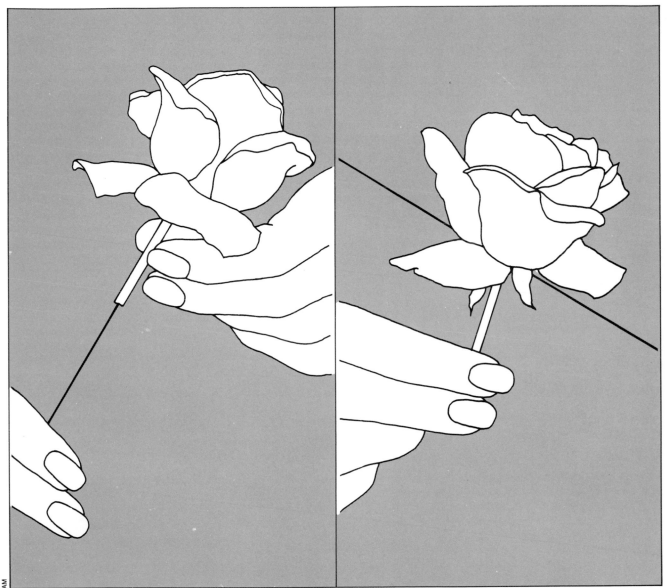

Flowers must be wired before they can be dried face-up in desiccant. Cut natural stem close to the flower head, leaving a one inch stub. Insert a wire up stem, part way into the head of the flower. For flowers with woody, impenetrable, or very thin stems, it is sometimes preferable to wire through the calyx, crosswise.

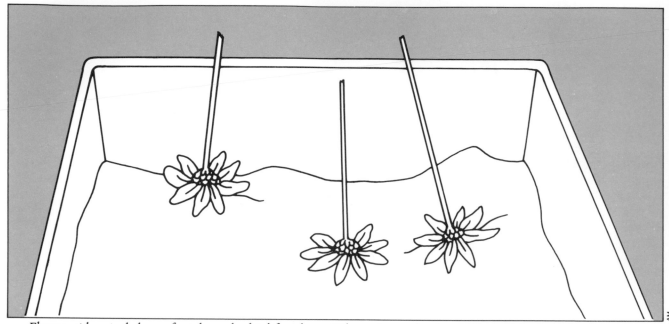

Flowers with a single layer of petals can be dried face down. When using sand or borax, place them in open boxes. It is not necessary to wire flowers with strong natural stems—just leave the stems sticking up out of the medium.

technique, the sand does not actually draw out the moisture from the petals. It is not, in the literal sense, a desiccant; it merely holds the petals in a lifelike position while the moisture evaporates naturally. The flowers will dry in three to five weeks, depending on the thickness and number of petals, and the warmth and dryness of the atmosphere.

In this method you can also use a mixture of borax and cornmeal as the drying medium. The recommended proportion varies: One part borax to three or four of cornmeal is effective, but more or less of either seems to make little difference. Mix thoroughly and be sure there are no lumps.

Any sturdy, open container, such as a shoe box, can be used—the size will depend on the flowers you are drying and how many you dry at one time. Be sure the container doesn't leak. In general, it is a

good idea to keep all of one variety of flower in one box; in a mixed box, it is hard to know when each of the different flowers are ready.

Flowers with only a single row of petals, such as rudbeckia or wild carrot, can be dried face-down in the medium. Pour one to two inches of sand or borax-cornmeal mixture into the box. Lay the flower on the sand so that the petals are in a natural position and are in contact with the sand at all points. (To dry a flower with a prominent center, like echinea, make an indentation for the center first.) You can place flowers in the box until the surface is covered, but be sure the flowers don't touch or overlap. When all flowers are in position, slowly pour more sand in the box to cover them. All parts of the flower must be in contact with the sand. Allow the sand to trickle in through your fingers; this will help ensure that there are no lumps and that

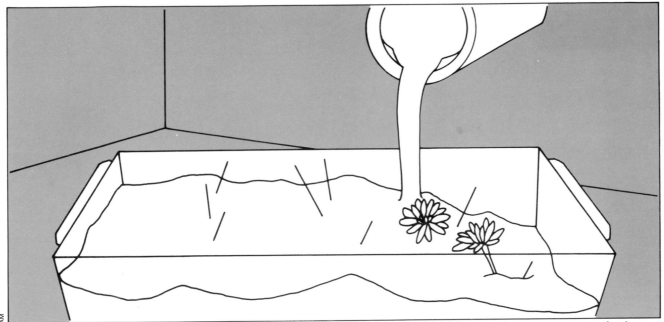

Slowly sift drying medium around and over flowers so that all petals are surrounded and the natural shape is maintained. Flowers drying face-up in silica gel are wired on short stems which are bent to fit inside the sealed tin.

all the tiny cracks between the petals are filled. The flowers should be completely covered with at least an inch or two of sand.

With flowers that are dried face down in sand, the natural stem can remain sticking out of the box. If, however, the stem is thick, soft, or fleshy, it is better to replace it with a wire stem and add a false stem later. For flowers with a hollow stem, like zinnias, the wire can be inserted through the natural stem into the head of the flower. Again, be careful not to push the wire through the flower—it will stick out when the flower dries and shrinks.

Flowers with several layers of petals; flowers, like many dahlias, with petals that are curled up or cupped; or flowers, like a hybrid tea rose, with an upright rather than flat shape; all these must be dried face-up in sand or borax. This means, first of all, that they cannot be dried with their natural stems—they

must be wired before they are dried. After the flower is dried it is almost impossible to insert a wire without shattering it, and it is very difficult to add a false stem to a flower that is not wired. Wire the flower as explained in the previous section on air-drying. A six- to eight-inch piece of 24 to 21 gauge wire is the most convenient; use the heavier weight—the lower number—for larger flowers.

Cover the bottom of the drying box with two inches of sand or a borax-cornmeal mixture. Bend the wire stem at a sharp upward angle just below where it emerges from the stalk of the real stem. Settle the flower—face up, stem down—in the sand and begin to pour in more sand to cover it. Be careful to fill every part of the flower; lift the upper layers of petals with a toothpick or brush and sift the sand between the petals. Continue until all parts of the flower are covered.

For flowers like tulips and roses, with a deep cup shape, it may be easier to place each flower in a separate paper or plastic cup. Great care must be taken to keep the level of the sand equal both inside and around the outside of the flower, in order to keep from distorting the shape. Most long spikes of flowers, like delphinium, can be dried lengthwise in long boxes. These require no special care except that you must sift the sand carefully so that one side does not become flattened.

It is a good idea to have one flower in each box placed so that it can be removed easily to check the progress of the drying, especially if the box contains large, complicated specimens. It is a terrific nuisance to uncover everything and have to bury it all again. It will not damage the flowers at all to be left in the sand or borax-cornmeal mixture until you are ready to arrange them. However, if you need to reuse the boxes and the sand, the flowers can be removed and stored while others are processed. Begin by uncovering one flower to check if it is dry; every part of it must be crisp and stiff. To uncover the rest, tilt the box and begin slowly to pour off the sand from one corner. As the flowers begin to appear from the sand, lift them gently from the box. One easy way to store the finished flowers is to stick the wires (or stems) into blocks of Styrofoam. They can also be placed on a wire mesh screen with their stems hanging down (as described for drying wild carrot).

Both the sand and the borax-cornmeal mixture can be reused indefinitely. The media should be sifted before they are used again to remove any broken petals or flower parts, and any lumps should be broken up.

Long stalks of material, such as delphinium, are placed lengthwise in boxes. Carefully sift the medium in and around the individual blossoms to insure that the flowers on the underside of the stalk are not crushed or flattened.

Drying Chemicals

IN RECENT YEARS COMMERCIAL DRYING MEDIA HAVE been introduced to the market. These are all made from some form of silica gel—the crystal powder used to line cookie or biscuit tins and camera cases to ensure dryness and prevent mildew. The crystals draw moisture from the air and absorb it. When in contact with the petals of a flower, they will draw the moisture from them.

When they first became available, commercial desiccants—sold under such names as "Flower Dry" and "Flower Keep"—were declared a great advance in the drying of flowers. It became possible to dry flowers in a matter of days, rather than weeks. A much wider range of flowers could be dried, and much truer and more vivid colors could be obtained. However, the popularity of desiccants has waned somewhat as their drawbacks have become more apparent. Now it is difficult to find them on the market; when available, they are usually sold in craft stores and are also offered by mail order supply sources (see Sources, page 140).

In general, the desiccant silica gel is applied in the same way as the sand or borax-cornmeal mix. The flowers are buried completely, face up or face down, depending on the form. However, there are several important differences to remember.

The container used must be completely airtight, so a sealed tin is best because otherwise the silica will absorb moisture from the air. All the flowers must be wired on short wires bent to fit in the tin.

Flowers will dry very quickly in silica—most in five to ten days, but the timing is different for each kind of flower, and flowers left in the medium for too long will fade rapidly and soon disintegrate. Great attention must be paid to every stage of the drying process and experimentation is necessary to obtain the best result.

Flowers dried in silica are often not stable. Because of the light weight of the crystals and the speed of the drying process, arrangers are tempted to

Paper or plastic cups are useful for drying short, thick stalks or for flowers with a deep cuplike shape, such as tulips.

dry a wide variety of flowers, some of which simply are not everlastings. Unless these flowers are kept in conditions of very low humidity, they reabsorb moisture from the air and go limp soon after being removed from the drying container. These flowers can be used in museums, in rooms with carefully controlled temperature and humidity, or under glass domes, but for the average arranger they are a waste of time.

Because the silica absorbs the moisture from the flowers, the crystals must be dried again before reuse. Most of the commercial varieties have special indicator crystals that turn color when they need to be dried. Crystals are dried by placing them in a low-temperature oven for several hours.

Despite these drawbacks—and the additional disadvantage that these media are quite expensive (much more so than sand or borax)—silica-dried flowers have much more vivid colors, and the flower will have a more lifelike appearance than those dried in other media, as long as the silica is used by experienced hands.

It is another great advantage to be able to have the flowers dried in a matter of days, rather than weeks. The process can be speeded up even more by placing the tins in a low-temperature oven for several hours, or by placing the flowers and medium in an ovenproof container in a microwave oven for an even shorter time period. Needless to say, great care must be taken with the timing of these procedures.

After the flowers are removed from the silica, it is important to keep them stored in low humidity until you are ready to use them, especially if you are drying in a climate where natural humidity levels are high. Often it is best to put them back in a sealed tin with a small quantity of silica to preserve their dryness. Make sure the petals are not in contact with this silica, or it will continue to draw moisture from them and the colors will fade.

To reiterate, the preparation of flowers for drying with any of the methods listed—sand, borax-cornmeal or a desiccant—is identical. The flowers must be in perfect condition, with no blemishes or insect damage. They must be turgid; it is almost impossible to place a flower with limp, floppy petals in a lifelike position. It is best to use flowers straight from the garden—pick a few at a time and bury them in the medium at once. If this is not possible, the flowers should be conditioned immediately after harvesting. Cut the stems and place them in warm water, then leave them for several hours in a cool, dark place. Many wild flowers will wilt soon after they are picked but can be reconditioned with warm water. Be careful not to let the flower heads get wet.

A reminder: Flowers must be harvested at the proper moment, usually just before they come into full bloom. For this reason, and because it is hard to know if the flowers are completely fresh, these methods do not work well for flowers bought from florists.

After the flowers are removed from the medium, they may still have a powdery residue on the petals. This can be removed with a dry, soft watercolor brush. Broken petals can be replaced with a milk-based glue diluted with water. Some books recommend gluing petals in place before the flowers are dried. This can be effective for flowers with a single layer of petals, like tulips, but in general it is a messy nuisance. Flowers that tend to drop their petals aren't a good drying choice anyhow; they are not usually worth the effort to avoid the inevitable breakage.

For other suggestions about storage and grooming after drying, as well as for information about attaching stems, see Chapter Six, page 125.

Glycerine for Foliage

MOST PLANT FOLIAGE DOES NOT DRY WELL. Chlorophyll is one of the most perishable of plant materials; when it breaks down, the green color disappears. Much material that can be air-dried is used as a filler to replace foliage—there are many types of dried arrangements that do not need green

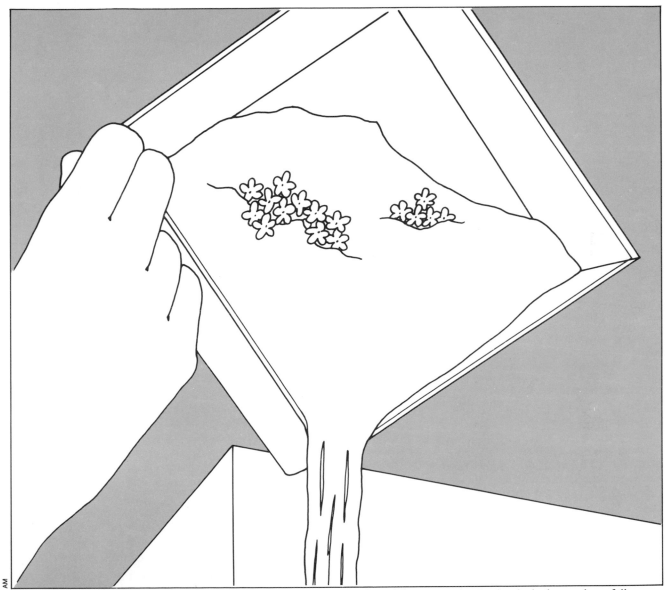

Remove one flower first to check if all the contents of a container are dry. If they are ready, slowly tilt the box and carefully pour the medium from one corner into another tin. As flowers emerge from the medium, gently lift them out and set them aside. Never pull flowers hastily while they are still covered—the weight of the medium will break off the petals.

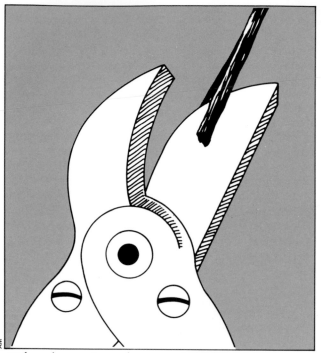

Make a deep cut in woody stems to be treated with glycerine—the branch and foliage will take up the solution more readily.

leaves as their base. However, there may be some kinds of foliage you would like to use, and there are several ways of preparing them.

The first method involves glycerine. This chemical can be purchased in liquid form from a chemist or drug-supply wholesaler. It is used to treat mature, leafy foliage—either entire branches, such as beech or magnolia, or individual leaves, such as ivy or aspidistra. The branches must be picked in midseason—after the leaves have opened completely and while they are still filled with fluid. Remove all leaves from the lower section of the branch and any damaged or withered leaves, then prune to obtain the most desirable outline. Make a three or four inch split in the bottom of the stem with a pruning shears to insure the best intake of the solution (some people prefer to pound the stems with a hammer). One part of glycerine is mixed with two or three parts near-boiling water. Stand the branches in several inches of the solution—take care to use a heavy, upright container for the solution, so it won't tip over. The branches will have to absorb the solution for two to six weeks, depending on the texture of the leaves and the heaviness of the branch. Check often to see if you need to add more solution to the container; if you add more solution, it does not need to be hot. As the branches dry, the leaves will turn various shades of brown, ranging from gold to glossy green-brown to almost black. The procedure is finished when all parts of the leaves have turned color. The leaves may exude excess solution from their pores; wipe this away before using them in an arrangement, or they will stain or damage any surface on which they may fall.

One great advantage to foliage treated in this manner is the resulting texture. The leaves become leathery, flexible, and easy to handle. They also last almost indefinitely in this form. If they become dusty, they can be wiped clean with a damp cloth.

Sometimes people think that this method will work to treat colorful autumn foliage. Unfortunately, this is not the case. The leaves and branches must still be taking moisture up through their stems in order to absorb the solution; autumn foliage is no longer doing this, and the leaves will simply drop from the branches.

Even when done mid-season with the right kinds of branches, this method is somewhat unpredictable. Often the branches will not take up the solution. The only thing to do is to start over with a reheated solution and new material. Small, single leaves or vines can be treated by completely submersing them in the solution. Use a thicker half-water, half-glycerine solution for these. When the leaves have turned color—it usually takes two to three weeks—remove them and wipe off the excess solution.

Beech, magnolia, maple, hornbeam, elaeagnus, and leucothoe are among the best branches to try with the glycerine preparation. Eucalyptus responds very well, and is often sold prepared this way. The foliage of baptisia, when it responds to treatment, will turn gun-metal grey, almost black. All of these, of course, will require experimentation to determine the exact length of time required by each species.

Pressing

THERE IS ANOTHER METHOD FOR DRYING FOLIAGE which, while it will not produce the same effects as the glycerine procedure, is not so uncertain, time-consuming, and messy. Certain types of foliage can be pressed and dried. Pressing is also a method for drying flowers, but the resulting flowers can only be used to create flat, two-dimensional flower pictures. Pressed foliage can be used in these, but can also provide a variety of material for arrangements.

Pressing works most effectively with foliage that is fairly flat in its natural state. For instance, ferns can be handled well this way, particularly the ones with a heavy, leathery texture. The flat forms of juniper, especially the florist's western cedar, also yield good results. The long, swordlike leaves of iris, gladiolus, or montbretia press well. This method is also effective with some autumn foliage material; if small sprays of leaves are dried, ensure that the leaves will not fall off by gluing the joints between leaf and stem and allowing the glue to dry before pressing.

It is unnecessary, indeed even harmful, to press these leaves under a great weight. Simply spread several sheets of newspaper on the floor or on any flat surface; lay several leaves on the paper, taking care they do not overlap; cover them with more newspaper, then more foliage. Continue to make a pile, alternating layers of paper and leaves. The newspaper is absorbent enough to keep the leaves from developing mildew, and the loose arrangement of the pile will allow sufficient air circulation. This method will also help you avoid the stiff two-dimensional look of most material dried under a

A traditional flower press alternates layers of wood and blotting paper. Tighten the wing nuts to apply pressure.

weight. Some curving of the stems will still be possible. It is, of course, impossible to avoid some stiffness; material dried this way must be combined skillfully with other fillers that distract from the flatness. Also, much of this material is very delicate and must be handled with care.

Pressing should be done in a warm, dry place; under good conditions leaves should be dry in several weeks, depending on the thickness of the leaf. Check periodically, lifting the leaves to be sure they don't stick to the surface of the paper.

Flowers for dried flower pictures or flat decoration can be pressed in a flower press or between sheets of blotting paper under a weight. Take care that the blotting paper has no textured surface that will show up on the surface of the flower.

Chapter Five

The Everlastings Catalogue

THE EVERLASTING CATALOGUE PRESENTS SOME of the best known and some of the least familiar drying plants. The obvious essentials are mentioned as well as ideas about unexpected possibilities. Keep in mind that every locale is unique; some of the wild plants mentioned will be common everywhere, some available in only to a few areas. You can create beautiful arrangements with a small fraction of the plants listed—don't be disappointed if some are unknown or unavailable. This catalogue is to introduce you to at least a few new and unusual flowers that you can grow, know, and enjoy. Consider these as starting points to your own explorations. The genus, species, then family for each plant is listed at the beginning of the entry. Use this botanical information to find plants that are similar, that are related, or that can be used in the same way.

There are many more flowers that can be dried with silica than just those listed. Experiment with the ones mentioned here, then go on from there—this is not a technique for everyone. Often, several drying methods can be used for a given plant—the choice will depend on your personal preference and the result you desire. In general, sand and a borax-cornmeal combination are interchangeable, so both will not be listed.

Acacia

A. armata, A. decurrens, etc.; Leguminosae

The most familiar species of this flower is known as the mimosa to most florists. The fragrant, fluffy yellow flowers are a welcome, refreshing addition to bouquets throughout the winter and early spring. Both the flowers and the grey-green foliage air-dry rapidly, and can either be hung or allowed to dry in graceful curves while standing in water or in arrangements. There are a number of other, less-familiar acacias sold as foliage material; most of them air-dry easily and provide long, sweeping, slightly exotic lines to arrangements. Most of the acacias can be grown only in a semi-tropical climate.

MC

Achillea

A. millefolium, A. tomentosa,
A. ptarmica, etc.; Compositae

There are both well-known wildflowers and garden favorites in this genus, and many varieties are excellent for drying. Coronation Gold, with its long, strong stems and large, bright heads of unfading chrome yellow, is probably the most familiar. There are also many lovely rock-garden species that are easily grown and are more interesting. The pink varieties, while pretty in the herb garden, are the least successful for drying. *A. ptarmica* includes such varieties as Angel's Breath and The Pearl; these are clusters of small, white, round, double flowers that dry very well. Hang and air-dry all species after removing the leaves.

Allium
Amaryllidaceae

There are probably 500 species in the vast genus of onions. Many of the hardy bulbs make easily grown, attractive plants in the garden and also provide excellent cut flowers and drying material. The only reason they are not more widely grown is the ridiculous objection that they smell like, well, onions. *A. giganteum* is indeed a giant—four to five feet tall in the garden—and is available from florists in the early summer. Some of the smaller species, such as *A. moly,* a lovely, bright-yellow flower, or *A. senescens glauca,* a late-blooming plant with fascinating swirls of grey foliage, are perfect for the rock garden, although they may be grown easily anywhere. Even the culinary types of allium can be dried—leeks have a beautiful flower, and chives bloom with masses of pink-purple blossoms in early spring. All the alliums can be air-dried, but most dry best if allowed to stand upright with their stems in a small amount of water; the result is a more open, natural shape to the head.

AM

Amaranthus

A. caudatus; A. tricolor;
Amaranthaceae

This half-hardy annual has a florid Victorian name that matches its appearance: Love-lies-bleeding. It is a large, ungainly plant with long, interesting hanging blossoms. The seeds are widely available and should be started early indoors, since this is a tropical family sensitive to frost. Pick it when about half the flowers on the stalk are open and the rest are still tight. Remove all the leaves before drying. Hang the stems to air-dry, or stand them upright in a small amount of water. There are wild amaranthuses which are tempting to dry, but they shatter easily and are extremely prickly and scratchy, so it is best to ignore them.

AM

Anaphalis

A. margaritacea; Compositae

Pearly everlasting is a pretty wildflower of North America and Europe, and can also be grown as a rock-garden plant. It makes mats of bright silvery-white foliage in rocky fields and old pastures. Its flowers are clusters of white, round papery petals which bloom in August and should be picked before the centers of the flowers have opened completely. Some arrangers favor anaphalis for spraying or dyeing in various ways. Strip off the leaves and hang the stems to air-dry.

Armeria

A. maritima; Plumbaginaceae

Close examination of the sea-pink, or thrift, reveals its resemblance to some species of the perennial statice, to which it is related; in fact, for a long time the plant was classified as *Statice armeria*. A hardy perennial, it is found growing wild on cliffs along the British coast; because of its tolerance of salt spray, it is a nice addition to the seaside garden. In America it is widely available as a rock-garden plant. Hang the stems to air-dry.

Artemesia
A. albula, A. absinthium;
Compositae

Besides the lovely silvery foliage plants used for drying, this genus also includes the herbs tarragon and wormwood (as well as the common allergenic weed mugwort). Silver King and Silver Queen—the most widely available varieties—are old garden favorites and can frequently be found persistently growing in abandoned farmyards and around old houses. It is an extremely hardy perennial. The flowers of all members of this genus are inconspicuous but make an attractive spire of silver in fresh or dried arrangements. Pick it in late August; strip off only the soiled bottom leaves; hang the stems to air-dry.

Asclepias

A. tuberosa, A. syriaca;
Asclepiadaceae

The asclepias, or orange butterfly-weed, is one of North America's most beautiful and dramatic wildflowers. Since it is a protected plant in many states, you should grow it in the garden for picking; it makes an excellent hardy garden perennial and is grown easily from seed. The brilliant orange flowers are best dried in silica. They fade quickly when exposed to direct light. The elegant pointed pods of *A. tuberosa* (which has the attractive regional nickname of railroad Annie), as well as the large boat-shaped pods of the common milkweed (*A. syriaca*) are also useful dried materials. Harvest them *after* the innumerable silky seeds have been released.

AM

Astilbe

A. astilboides, A. chinensis; Saxifragaceae

This perennial is shade tolerant and it also grows well in damp soil. The feathery plumes are available in red, pink, and white shades. They shrink considerably when air-dried, so borax or silica procedures are best. The foliage is also ornamental and can be pressed. Aruncus is an enormous relative of the astilbe, with tall white or cream flowers that can be dried in the same way.

Astrantia

A. major; Umbelliferae

Both the Latin and vernacular name, starwort, of this pretty perennial refer to its star-like appearance. Although an old-fashioned garden plant in England, astrantia is now being sold by florists in North America during the early and mid-summer. The delicate silvery beauty of this plant is best displayed in small-scale arrangements or wreaths. Strip the leaves and hang the stems to dry.

Baccharis

B. halimifolia; Compositae

Baccharis is a native shrub of the eastern American coastal areas and makes luxuriant silver masses—six to twelve feet high—in open marshes late in the autumn. The flowers are inconspicuous, but the white fluffy pappus of the seed can be dried. Pick them when they have just begun to appear; they shatter easily if left too long. Leave some of the silvery leaves on the stem, since they dry well. Stand the stiff stems upright.

Baptisia

B. australis; Leguminosae

The false indigo is a handsome perennial—glaucus blue-grey foliage topped by spires of lupinlike flowers. The flowers produce dramatic pods that turn almost black when ripe; pick them after the color is rich and dark. You do not need to hang these, since the stems are very strong. Spray the pods with varnish to deepen the color and give them a slight gloss. The foliage can be treated with glycerine in mid-summer.

Branches

We'll abandon Latin for a moment for a catchall category name. There are many trees and shrubs that provide useful and dramatic material for drying, and most of it can be picked in winter, when little else is available. Branches provide a large-scale outline for a big arrangement, but they can be cut to almost any size. *Liquidamber styraciflua,* the beautiful American sweet gum, and *Euonymus alatus* both have fascinating corky wings on the bark. *Salix babylonica,* the weeping willow, makes sweeping curves of bright yellow when picked in late winter; the flexible twigs can be shaped into tight curves and will dry that way. *Salix matsudana tortuosa,* the corkscrew willow, and *Corylus contorta* both dry in fantastic twisted stalks. During winter walks, use your imagination and look for interesting galls, dead branches covered with lichens, or an abandoned nest.

AM

Capsicum

C. frutescens; Solanaceae

Late autumn marks the appearance of the splendid hot peppers in the markets. Whether sold as vegetables, cut ornamental material, or as pot plants, the brilliant fruits add countless color and shape combinations to fall decor. Originally perennial plants found in Central and South America, these peppers can be grown as annuals, although they need a fairly long growing season and a lot of sun. The brightest orange and red shades dry the best; the fruit will shrink and shrivel, but that only adds to their interest. They can be air-dried, either hanging on their original stems or separately, spread on a screen.

Carthamus

C. tinctorius; Compositae

It is a surprise to many that the safflower is a very handsome and easy-to-grow annual; perhaps because of its importance in the production of oil and dye we expect something much less ornamental. This flower has become quite popular with florists in the past few years and is now widely available during the summer and fall. Or you can grow it yourself—the seeds are offered in most seed catalogues, and it is a great addition to the herb garden. Pick it when some of the flowers are open and some are still in bud. Hang it to air-dry. Retain some of the leaves near the tops of the stems, since they are spiky and attractive.

Catananche

C. caerulea; Compositae

The pretty cupid's dart—with its blue, chicory-like flowers and silvery bracts—lines roadsides in southern France. It is, unfortunately, somewhat more difficult to grow in a northern climate. Most gardeners grow it as an annual, starting seed early indoors, but in the rock garden or on a terrace with good drainage it might persist from year to year. The papery silver bracts can be harvested after the petals have faded; the flower itself can be dried in borax or silica.

61

Celastrus

C. orbiculatus, C. scandens;
Celastraceae

The brilliant orange and gold of the American bittersweet brightens the landscape in the late fall; for many of us it is as much a sign of autumn as turning leaves. Although it was protected from picking in some areas years ago, most bans have now been lifted since this rampant vine can become a nuisance if it is not controlled. It is best picked after the large, ungainly leaves have dropped naturally (otherwise they must be tediously stripped by hand) but before the orange outer shell has opened. The shells will open as they dry and will stay on the stem; if the vine is picked after the shells have opened, they will drop. If possible, it is best to arrange bittersweet immediately after cutting it; allow it to dry in the arrangement and it will hold up much better. *C. orbiculatus* is the Chinese bittersweet, often sold as an ornamental vine; the berries are larger but grow more sparsely on the stem than the native species.

Celosia

C. argentea var. cristata, plumosa; Amaranthaceae

These late-summer annuals are usually described as "enormous red brains"; this is not an unfair description, although they are not always enormous and also come in shades of gold and pink. The bloom on the bottom right is the coxcomb type and certainly is a dramatic focal point in an arrangement. Smaller sections can be broken off for small-scale work. The plumosa varieties are the tall feathery celosias; they also come in a range of red-gold colors. Both types are tender annuals and can be grown from seeds; start them early indoors. Harvest them for drying before they begin to produce their innumerable black seeds; strip the leaves from the stems and hang. The colors fade considerably after drying, producing more subtle, attractive shades. Both celosias are very inexpensive and readily available from florists in August and September.

MC

Centaurea

C. macrocephala, C. moschata, C. montana, etc.; Compositae

A genus of some 500 species, centaurea includes both good garden material and numerous wildflowers, many useful for drying. In its general shape, the centaurea resembles a thistle, to which it is related, but it has no thorns. *C. macrocephala* is a striking perennial in the garden—a large tuft of yellow petals emerges from what looks like a bright chestnut wig. The sweet sultan and bachelor's button are familiar and easy-to-grow hardy annuals. All can be air-dried while hanging; the bachelor's buttons shrink, so try drying them in borax. The calyxes—the part remaining after the petals and seeds have dropped—are pretty and star-like; pick them late in the season.

Chrysanthemum
C. morifolium, C. parthenium;
Compositae

Very few of the innumerable hybrid florist and garden "mums" dry well—they either turn unattractive colors or the petals shatter when dry. The best of the common florist types are the small tight yellow buttons. *C. parthenium* (matricaria or feverfew) resembles this type, but has many small white heads on a stalk. This plant is an old garden favorite, a biennial that self-sows freely and blooms prolifically throughout the summer. The flowers can be dyed systemically before drying or sprayed with color afterward. Remove the leaves from the stems and hang them to dry.

Clematis

C. vitalba, etc.; Ranunculaceae

The hundreds of beautiful species of clematis all have silky, whorled seed heads although the arrangement and number varies greatly. If allowed to dry naturally, the heads become fluffy and white, with a tendency to fall away if not handled carefully. They can be dipped in a thin varnish to preserve the silky look. Long strands of seed heads can be stretched along string to preserve the sweep of the curves.

Cytisus

C. scoparius; etc.; Leguminosae

Scotch broom is an attractive shrub, easily grown in mild climates. Unfortunately, it is a difficult plant to grow north of Zone 5, but since it is a staple product of florists, you don't need to grow it yourself. The long dark-green stems make strong, sweeping outlines in either fresh or dried arrangements. Broom dries a dark grey-green color but can be lightly sprayed with floral paint for a more life-like green.

Dahlia

D. pinnata, D. merckii, etc.; Compositae

This late-summer plant is one of the best to dry with Silica. Some varieties can be grown as annuals from seed, but most are produced by a fleshy tuber that is lifted from the earth each winter. The small- to medium-sized varieties are most successful and offer a wide range of colors. Insert wires in the blooms and place them face-up in the medium. Dahlias dry best straight from the garden.

Datura

D. stramonium; Solanaceae

The decadent lily-like trumpets of Jimsonweed advertise the narcotic qualities of the plant, and the sprays of spiny seedpods smell of the plant's powerful alkaloids. But, datura makes a striking addition to any large-scale arrangement. It is a tender annual of the tropics, but can be grown naturally in waste areas from Zone 5 south. Strip the leaves from the stems and stand the pods upright to air-dry. All parts are poisonous.

Daucus

D. carota; Umbelliferae

The wild carrot, or Queen Anne's lace, is one of the prettiest and best known of the umbelliferae, a family that produces many plants for drying. Queen Anne's lace is abundant almost everywhere in the late summer, particularly along roadsides and in waste areas. It is one of the most successful subjects for drying with borax, but it can also be air-dried on a wire screen, with the head flat, facing upward on the screen and the stem hanging straight below through the mesh. (This method is explained and illustrated on page 35.) The interesting bird's nests made by the flowers when they have finished blooming are also good dried material.

Delphinium

D. grandiflorum, etc.; Ranunculaceae

We will present the annual and perennial species of this genus separately because both deserve separate illustrations and they have quite different habits of growth. Both are invaluable as dried flowers. The species named above are some of the perennial forms, although most of the gorgeous varieties listed in catalogues are a confusing assortment of hybrids. Delphiniums are one of the essentials of a great summer border, and while they are not carefree, low-maintenance plants, they are unequivocally worth the effort they require. Very deep, rich soil is essential to grow them, with extra feeding every year. They flourish in a climate of long days and cool nights. The perennial species dry beautifully in silica or borax (the colors are preserved more vividly in the former), but can also be hung to air-dry if picked when the spike of flowers is half open, half in bud. The lovely *D. chinensis* is completely different—a small plant suitable for the rock garden with wonderfully vivid blue flowers that dry well in silica or borax. It will bloom the first year from seed.

MC

Delphinium

D. ajacis, D. consolida;
Ranunculaceae

These are the annual forms of delphinium, usually called larkspur. They are much easier to grow than the perennials, since they demand less in special soil conditions. Larkspur self-sows freely, and even though the choice hybrids will eventually revert to the less-impressive species forms, all are lovely in the garden and good for drying or cutting. Larkspur air-dries very well—cut it when the blossoms are half open, half in bud. They come in a variety of colors, including blue and lavender, but the bright pinks are especially attractive. Strip the leaves from the stem and hang them to dry or preserve them in silica or borax. Keep in mind that all species of delphinium, like their near relative aconitum, are poisonous if ingested.

Dictamnus

D. albus; Rutaceae

The beautiful gas plant is so called because of the numerous tiny oil glands that cover the upper flower spike and seedpods. These glands give off a gas that will ignite with a flash along the entire stem if a match is touched to it. This does not harm the plant at all; in fact, dictamnus, when it is established, is an almost indestructible perennial. It makes a handsome, shrub-like brush of dark-green leaves topped with three-foot spikes of pink or white orchid-like flowers. These blooms are followed by fascinating star-shaped seedpods. The seeds are ejected by a powerful spring mechanism in the pod. If you pick the pods before the seeds are gone, the seeds will be shot across the room.

Dipsacus
D. fullonum; Dipsacaceae

Be well-protected when you pick teasels for they are heavily armed with spikes, hooks, and prickles. Remove the leaves and scrape the prickles off the stems with a knife as you pick them—it's even more difficult to handle them after they are dry. Pick them when in flower to preserve the silvery tones of the stems and heads. Teasels are wild throughout Europe and North America. Let them air-dry hanging upside down.

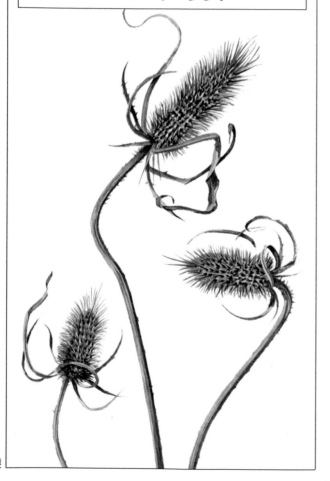

Echinocystis
E. lobata; Cucurbitaceae

The wild cucumber vine is a native northeastern annual vine found in damp thickets and along streams. The pretty sprays of white flowers and maple-shaped leaves are attractive but arrangers chiefly prize its feather-light seedpods surrounded by coiled tendrils. The pods can be harvested in the early autumn after they ripen. The stems are very weak— drape the tendrils around stronger material.

Echinops

E. exaltatus, syn. E. ritro; Compositae

Although its vernacular name is globe thistle, this is not, in fact, a thistle. Echinops is a very hardy perennial which is easily air-dried by hanging; leave a few leaves near the flower head to dry to a nice silver. The prickly heads look almost identical before and after they bloom so watch carefully for the best time to harvest them—as soon as the central globes are deep grey-blue and before the tiny flowers have appeared.

Epilobium

E. angustifolium; Onagraceae

This striking wildflower, often called fireweed, flourishes in burned over areas and in bare, rocky ground. Pick the tall spikes before the seedpods have opened and coiled into a tangled mass of spirals and seeds. A short species of epilobium thrives around streams and ponds; the flowers are insignificant, but the golden curls of its seed heads are an excellent filler. Harvest this one after the first hard frost.

Eryngium

E. maritimum, E. alpinum,
E. planum, etc.; Umbelliferae

This is another prickly blue-grey garden perennial, but unrelated to echinops, thistles, or holly, despite its common name of sea holly. One of the most surprising features of this plant is its bright silver-blue stems, which look as if they have been spray-painted. Eryngium species are found wild throughout Britain and the Continent, and there is even a wild American species. Also, both echinops and eryngium are available from florists throughout the summer. But, seeds and plants are available to gardeners, and it is a very easy plant to grow. Air-dry it while hanging.

Eucalyptus

E. globulus, etc.; Myrtaceae

The strong-scented, sticky Australian gums are familiar to all flower arrangers; they are a florist's wintertime staple. Several species are available fresh: the best-known, cork eucalyptus; Baby Blue, a miniature, bluer hybrid of the cork type; flat eucalyptus or silver dollar, with flat round leaves on red stems bearing numerous buds and flower clusters. Any of these can be dried in their natural state, or treated with glycerine. Most of the eucalyptus sold dried has been treated; this accounts for the stronger smell and leathery flexibility of the leaves and stems. It is also frequently dyed or spray-painted—the silver dollar is lovely for Christmas arrangements when frosted gold.

AM

Eupatorium

E. purpureum, E. cannabinum, E. perfoliatum, etc.; Compositae

This genus contains several familiar wildflowers of North America, at least one of which is naturalized throughout Britain. The tall purple joe-pye weed can be found blooming in August along streams and small ponds. It is important to pick this plant before the flowers have opened; once the fluffy individual florets have started to open, they will shatter when dried. Boneset is another species in this group, with white mounds of flowers that are similar to joe-pye weed. It grows in a damp habitat, often near joe-pye weed, and can be recognized by the interesting way the entire leaf surrounds the stalk. Pick boneset as you would joe-pye weed. Strip all the leaves from the stems and hang them to dry.

Ferns

Osmundaceae, Polypodiaceae, etc.

It is unfortunate that there is little drying material from the deep woods, but shade gardeners find some consolation in the fact that ferns can be dried. The tough-textured, leathery types like the evergreen Christmas ferns or the florist's leather-leaf dry best. Some of the finer species, however, add a delicate touch to miniature arrangements, and all are beautiful backgrounds for pressed-flower pictures. Ferns can easily be pressed between layers of newspapers. It is not necessary to place a heavy weight on them. Dry the hay-scented fern just as it is turning gold in the fall. All dried ferns are extremely fragile and require careful handling.

Gomphrena

G. globosa; Amaranthaceae

The globe amaranth resembles a brilliant purple or shocking pink clover and is often called that by non-botanical florists, who sell it in the late summer. It is a tender annual from the tropics, like its relative, love-lies-bleeding, and is easily grown from seed started early. There are attractive pale orange and golden shades available occasionally—these usually have longer and stronger stems than the purple varieties and can be hung to dry. The purple gomphrena is best cut from the natural stem and wired like strawflowers.

AM

Gramineae

The grass family

It would be futile to list even a few of the 400 genera (over 4,500 species) of grasses—almost all the Latin names are completely unfamiliar and the classification characteristics hopeless for amateurs to interpret. Luckily, most of us know more or less what a grass looks like, and almost all of them are excellent drying material, ranging from the enormous exotic plumes of the pampas or zebra grasses to the innumerable small, fluffy fillers like the hare's tail. There are also ornamental garden mixtures, both annual and perennial, available from seed catalogues, but with grasses so abundant on the roadsides it doesn't seem worthwhile to use garden space to grow them. If harvested early in the summer, the grasses will retain a soft silvery grey-green color; pick them later for gold and bronze shades. Grasses can be spread flat to dry or placed upright in tall containers. Just be sure to pick them before the seed heads start to shatter.

Gypsophila
G. paniculata; Caryophyllaceae

The lovely baby's breath has been much abused by incompetent florists, who stuff it indiscriminately into every shoddy center-piece or wedding bouquet in order to cover a multitude of sins. It is a pretty plant, either in the garden or in arrangements, but care should be taken to avoid the clichéd look associated with it. It is easily air-dried, either hanging or upright; trim off all the leaves and the countless broken stems, which distract from its airy lightness. The most familiar variety is the double Bristol fairy, but there are single types available too. These are hardy, summer-blooming perennials; there are also pretty annual gypsophilas, but they are not good for drying.

AM

Heather

Erica and *Calluna Species;*
Ericaceae

The heaths and heathers (all are called heathers by florists) are a mainstay of winter flower
arrangements. These lovely plants are natives
of Europe and can be found wild in many
parts of Britain, but are discouragingly difficult for North American gardeners to cultivate. However, a wonderful variety of
heather is available from florists during the
non-gardening months. Almost all species
dry well; the tiny needle-like foliage will
yellow and drop, but the flowers will remain.
Don't hang these (since the tiny bell-like
flowers would then face the wrong way);
simply stand them upright or allow them to
dry in arrangements. Heathers are excellent in
wreaths, too; arrange them before the stems
dry and become brittle.

Helianthus

H. annuus, H. tuberosus, etc.;
Compositae

The enormous annual sunflower is truly a flower of grand scale. Many flower arrangers are intimidated by its grandeur but it is certainly a dramatic focal point when used with a bold hand. There are numerous smaller-scale hybrids in a range of bronze and red-gold shades that are grown from seed as half-hardy annuals. In addition, quite a few wild North American species of brilliant yellow are available, including the Jerusalem artichoke, which has an edible tuberous root. The flowers can all be dried with borax or silica, and the huge seed heads of the giant type can be harvested either before or after the seeds have been removed.

Helichrysum
H. bracteatum; Compositae

The strawflower is certainly the best-known of the everlastings and is almost universally available dried from florists, especially in the fall. It is easy to grow from seed as a tender annual, although it is not a very attractive garden subject. The entire plant has thick stems that are out of proportion with the small flowers. The foliage, also not very attractive, is beset by a variety of insects and diseases, though the flowers are not usually affected. The flowers must be removed from the stems and wired before drying. Since fresh strawflowers are often sold inexpensively by florists throughout the summer, many arrangers prefer to buy them rather than grow them. The advantage of buying fresh ones and wiring them yourself is that a much more interesting array of colors is available, and the sizes range from giant heads to tiny delicate buds perfect for miniatures.

MC

Helipterum

H. roseum, H. manglesii;
Compositae

These species of everlastings and *Xeranthemum annuum* are known generally as acroclinium, roccardia, and rhodanthe, so there is much confusion in seed catalogues about what you are buying. All resemble helichrysm with their papery petals (which require little air-drying); like the strawflower, they are best wired before drying. They are usually available in white and shades of pink or deep rose; occasionally yellow species are offered. Helipterum species, characterized by brilliant yellow centers, are natives of Australia and South Africa. Xeranthemum have a more star-like appearance. All are easily grown, half-hardy annuals.

Herbs

This is an unfortunately vague catchall term—here it includes many of the culinary, medicinal, and ornamental foliage plants not discussed in other sections of this catalogue and not usually grown as cutting or border flowers. Herbs are, in general, easy to obtain and to grow and are often cultivated for their value in cooking or natural healing; rarely does the gardener realize the possibility of using them decoratively. Herbs include some of the earliest cultivated plants and are worth growing for their historical interest. Costmary, or bible leaf *(Chrysanthemum balsamita),* has small clumps of tansy-like flowers that bloom late in the autumn. *Ruta graveolens,* the common rue, has lovely bluish leaves, which can be pressed, and interesting clusters of square, box-like seedpods. The whole plant has a powerful medicinal smell that persists after drying. The mints offer a variety of foliage and flowers to dry; catnip (nepeta) has especially good grey foliage and flower heads, although it might tempt a cat to assault the arrangement. Experiment with any of the culinary herbs—they add a pleasing scent to a dried bouquet or wreath.

AM

Humulus

H. lupulus, H. americanus;
Cannabaceae

Vines add graceful, sweeping curves and flourishes to dried arrangements that no other material can provide; hops, in spite of the difficulties in handling them, are among the best of the vines. Look for them along roadsides, often clambering twelve to fifteen feet up trees and enveloping shrubs with their large grape-like leaves and golden, papery sheaves. The stems and leaves are equipped with abrasive, hooked prickles that enable the stems to climb—and to tear at the skin of would-be harvesters. Often, the best way to pick them is to cut an entire tree branch that is entwined with the hops. All leaves must be removed from the vine—a tedious job, but necessary to reveal the lovely curls of the stems and heads. Pick them in the fall as the hops start to turn gold. They smell strongly of beer and are soporific—hop pillows are made for insomniacs.

AM

Hydrangea
H. paniculata grandiflora,
H. macrophylla, etc.;
Saxifragaceae

These shrubs fall in and out of floral fashion. They were loved by the Victorians, abandoned, then revived by Constance Spry, reviled again, and are now swinging back as favorites. The lovely white forms are so useful—fresh, dried, and as landscaping material—it is hard to see why they were ever unpopular. (The lurid blue and purple varieties are another question.) The best species for drying is the peegee hydrangea, the woody shrub often grown as a small tree. This blooms for weeks in September and October and should be picked just as the heads begin to take on tinges of pink and gold and become drier to the touch. They can be used as fresh flowers, then saved to dry. The subtle shades of ivory and old-rose reflect all the most evocative, slightly decadent tones of autumn. The tender blue varieties can be dried with borax; it is best to break the enormous heads into smaller, more manageable clumps and wire each one separately.

AM

87

Iris

I. sibirica, I. japonica, I. pseudacorus, etc.; Iridaceae

Don't get your hopes up about drying the lovely flowers of this varied genus—they are among the most perishable of blossoms. They do, however, leave behind a fascinating array of seedpods to dry. If the tall bearded iris is not cut back it will occasionally form seeds, but most of these complicated hybrids are rarely fertilized. It is among the large assortment of species iris that we find the best and most prolifically produced pods. The Siberian iris makes slender capsules that open and arch back from the tip; they grow on long, strong stems and turn dark brown at the end of the season. The pods of the Japanese iris are round and turn a pale golden brown. *Iris pseudacorus,* the beautiful yellow water iris, produces enormous hanging capsules. These three species will flourish in a damp spot or ornament the edges of a small pond. Many of the other species will also yield capsules of interest; *Iris foetissima,* for example, while not noted for its bloom, yields a flamboyant arrangement of seeds.

Lavandula

L. officinalis; Labiatae

This is not one of the more conspicuous everlastings, but its warm pleasant smell is a wonderful addition to small bouquets and wreaths. It is also an old-fashioned sentimental favorite of many. If the flowers are going to be used for sachets, the strongest fragrance will result if the stalks are picked before the individual blossoms open. But if picked later, they still have quite a powerful scent and are slightly larger. The thick grey leaves, resembling rosemary, can also be used and contain the same fragrant oil.

Leontopodium

L. alpinum; Compositae

This fascinating alpine everlasting looks like a silvery, woolly starfish. Edelweiss is not a difficult plant to grow; like most alpines, its primary requirement is good drainage. Pick the flowers before the fluffy centers have begun to open or discolor. Leontopodium (which means lion's foot) can be dried best face-up on a wire screen. This is a protected European plant; should you encounter it in the Alps, don't touch it.

Liatris

L. spicata, etc.; Compositae

Originally native to North America, species of this genus have become popular garden subjects and invaluable cut flowers for the florist. The garden varieties vary in height from two to six feet and are easily grown and very hardy. The flowers are available year round from the florist and dry well if bought in good condition. Strip the leaves and hang the flowers to dry. Don't bother to dry the white varieties.

Limonium

L. latifolium, etc.; Plumbaginaceae

The names of the perennial forms of statice have been reclassified so many times that seeds and plants are called both limonium and statice. The native American sea lavender makes clouds of blue-purple in the north coastal salt marshes. This is a protected plant and should never be picked, but there are garden species that resemble it, and many kinds are sold by florists. All require no effort to dry.

Limonium

L. sinuatum, L. suworowii;
Plumbaginaceae

It seems as if no traditional arrangement is sold without annual statice. Remove it soon if you want to save it for drying. This annual can be easily grown if seed is started early; the same is true for *L. suworowii,* a perennial that will bloom in one summer if started early indoors. *L.sinuatum* stems have wing-like edges that should be stripped before hanging.

Lunaria
L. annua; Cruciferae

Honesty (money plant or pope's money) is for many of us the quintessential Victorian everlasting, and its translucent silver dollars are part of the decor of countless overstuffed parlors. It is surprising to find it was not introduced into America until the thirties. This is a member of the large family of mustards, many of which produce excellent pods for drying. In the case of the money plant, to quote horticulturist L. H. Bailey, it is the "thin, lustrous septa that are held in the pod-margins, like spectacles in their rims" that make the silver dollars. The exterior flaps of the pod will fall naturally if allowed to mature in the garden, but the best silvery color and texture is obtained if they are harvested when the pods start to turn brown and the exterior portion is then removed by hand. The plant is a biennial and will grow in some shade. It has pretty purple flowers very early in the spring.

AM

Marrubium

M. vulgare; Labiatae

Horehound is another of the aromatic herbs that can be used for flavor and fragrance as well as for visual interest in arrangements. The seed heads are arranged in knot-like clusters along the straight, grey stem accented with nubby grey foliage. While fresh, they can be shaped and tied into circles, and they make an interesting base for a wreath. To use them as an herb, gather the leaves and air-dry them; they make a strange-tasting, soothing throat medicine.

AM

Moluccella

M. laevis; Labiatae

The tiny flowers of this odd plant are almost invisible, hidden inside the large, green, shell-like bracts that give it the nickname bells of Ireland. Since it is a half-hardy annual needing a long season, it is often better to buy it than to grow it; it is sold intermittently throughout the year by florists. Only the mature bracts dry well—the smaller ones will shrivel—so pick or purchase the longest, fullest stems possible. The vivid green color fades to a creamy parchment. When dry, the bracts fall easily, so handle the stems with care or glue the individual shells back on the stalk. It can be air-dried or dried in sand or silica.

MC

Monarda

M. didyma, M. fistulosa; Labiatae

Another spectacular American native, bee balm makes flamboyant, shaggy heads of brilliant scarlet in the late summer. It is now a protected plant in the wild, but many lovely garden hybrids have been produced, though few rival the color of the original. It is unfortunate that little of the vibrance of the original red is left after drying, but even the remnants bring liveliness to arrangements. This is a member of the mint family, which will be noticeable from the strong, pleasant smell released when you touch it; another local name, Oswego tea, indicates how it has been used in the past. *M. fistulosa* is a much more common relative, and comes in a shade of lavender pink. Both can be air-dried.

Muscari

M. armeniacum; Liliaceae

It is easy to overlook many of the delicate pods produced by the earliest flowering bulbs; by the time these are going to seed, the rest of the garden is in full bloom and offers too many distractions. But these pods, as well as those of other small, early bloomers like *Fritillaria meleagris,* are lovely, subtle accents for small arrangements and are so numerous and easy to gather that you should be aware of them. The grape hyacinth is certainly one of the best-known spring flowers; it requiring almost no care or space; pods can be air-dried easily.

AM

Mustards

Capsella, Thlaspi, Hesperis, Erysimum, etc.; Cruciferae or Brassiciferae

We will abandon our Latin nomenclature momentarily to discuss this large family, the crucifers (named because the four-petaled flowers are in the shape of a cross; the family has been renamed Brassiciferae but crucifer conveys a truer sense of the plants). This family includes among its 3,000 species numerous plants of enormous value—all the vegetables related to the cabbage, for example—and quite a few lovely garden plants, but many of our most pervasive weeds are to be found here, too. Almost all these plants produce abundant and ornate seed capsules. Many are cold-weather plants, blooming in the early spring (those large fields of bright chrome yellow are filled with mustard), and the pods can be harvested in early summer. *Hesperis matronalis,* sweet rocket or dame's violet, is a nice garden biennial that blooms with tall stems of many purple flowers in the spring. The long, upright pods are often tinged purple. Field pennycress has almost circular capsules which dry a light gold brown. The vegetable species—radishes, watercress, etc.—yield seeds of interest. All the mustards provide invaluable filler.

Narcissus

Narcissus species, etc.;
Amaryllidaceae

It has probably not occurred to you to dry daffodils. These delightful harbingers of spring are so much a part of that season that they may seem out of place in an everlasting arrangement. Nevertheless, they dry excellently with desiccants and can be combined with other spring-like material in an effective bouquet. The varieties with the heaviest texture and most vivid color are the best, but the appealing miniature species are irresistible for tiny baskets or wreaths of moss.

MC

Nigella

N. damascena; Ranunculaceae

Love-in-a-mist is the delightful common name of this old-fashioned garden annual; the name is derived from the appearance of the delicate flower surrounded by the mist of the fine-cut, filmy foliage. The flower, usually blue or white, is an intricate composition of petals, stamens, and styles, followed by an even more wonderful inflated pod. The pods of the darker blue flowers are often streaked with red or purple. Pick them when the capsules have started to open at the top and scatter the seeds freely—this annual grows much better when self-sown. Leave some of the frilly foliage around the head to keep the misty look.

AM

Origanum
O. vulgare; Labiatae

Much confusion is caused by the various names of this plant and its relatives. Is it wild oregano or wild marjoram? It is not sweet marjoram or the herb oregano, which are annuals or tender perennials, although it is often sold as such, even by reputable sources. Although it resembles these herbs, the leaves, somewhat aromatic when fresh, have almost no flavor when dried. The flowers, however, make this hardy perennial worth growing; it can also often be found in the wild. It is actually the deep purple bracts surrounding the small pink blossoms which dry well, so pick it before the buds begin to open. Strip the leaves from the stems and air-dry the bracts.

AM

Ornithagalum

O. umbellatum, O. thyrsoides; Liliaceae

Neither the intimidating Greek of the botanical name nor the florists' tag of chincherinchee describe this flower well or endear it to flower arrangers. However, it is one of the longest lasting cut flowers—often two or three weeks in water—and can be dried successfully with desiccants. The florists' varieties are better suited to drying than the garden species, star of Bethlehem, which tends to close up when picked. This is one of the few flowers available from florists that dries better after it has opened in water. The individual florets open slowly along the stem; the stalk should be dried when approximately two-thirds of the florets are open.

MC

Paeonia

P. lactiflora, P. suffruticosa;
Paeoniaceae

This much-loved garden perennial competes with the rose for the title Queen of the Garden in May and June. The luxuriant, heavily scented flowers are so gorgeous it is almost impossible to go wrong in arranging them, and the trouble-free plants will outlive generations of gardeners. Peonies are a real challenge even to the dried-flower arranger who has become skilled with desiccants, but they are well worth the effort. The best results are obtained with the single or semi-double varieties of both the herbaceous and tree species, since it is much easier to insure that the silica surrounds all the petals—the huge, double varieties are practically impenetrable. The beautiful foliage of the tree peony can be pressed to dry.

Papaver

P. somniferum, P. rhoeas, P. orientale; also Glaucum, Argemone, etc.; Papaveraceae

Poppies in their many species are among the most perishable of flowers: some last scarcely half a day in the garden. However, they leave behind a fabulous assortment of delightful pods. Some, like the familiar perennial Oriental poppy, are arranged like intricate salt shakers, with perforated tops that release the seeds. The yellow horned poppy, *Glaucum flavum,* has lovely crinkled petals rapidly succeeded by a long, slender, curved, bean-like capsule often five to six inches in length. It is illegal to grow sizeable quantities of *P. somniferum,* the opium poppy, in the United States, but it is enjoyed in countless old-fashioned gardens by gardeners innocent of its more sinister aspects. Harvest it when the pods are mature; remove the leaves from the stem. The annual species will self-sow freely from year to year.

AM

Physalis

P. alkekengi; Solanaceae

The Chinese lantern, a member of the tomato or nightshade family, is among the most brilliantly colored autumn plants. When growing and flowering early in the season, the plants most resemble potatoes, another not very ornamental member of this group. No one would ever claim that physalis was a plant for the border; in fact, it should be grown in a far corner for it is quite invasive and weedy. It is a hardy perennial and spreads by underground runners so it is hard to eradicate once established. All its faults are forgiven, however, when the fiery orange lantern-shaped bladders appear in early autumn. Remove the leaves and air-dry; don't hang the stems upside down or the lanterns will hang the wrong way. Spread a small spot of clear glue where the lanterns join the main stem to keep them from falling off.

MC

Polygonum
P. cuspidatum, P. aubertii;
Polygonaceae

It is a nice surprise to find that even the hated Japanese knotweed has a redeeming virtue: It makes excellent dried material. Just don't make the mistake of letting it get started in your garden. Originally sold as an ornamental, this plant soon proved to be invasive and almost eradicable—it has established itself throughout North America. Pick it in the early autumn when the frothy white bloom is at its peak; remove the enormous leaves and hang to air-dry. The stems are often ten to twelve feet long and can make a wonderful frame for a large arrangement; you can use the small secondary branches for filler. The creamy color of the blooms change to golden brown if exposed to strong sunlight, but it is still attractive. The silver lace vine, which is sold as an ornamental, is also a polygonum and can be dried in late autumn.

Protea

Hakea, Banksia, Grevillea, etc.; Proteaceae

Unless you live in Australia, South Africa, or California, it's off to the florist for these exotics. The protea family is a large one—it includes such non-ornamentals as macadamia nuts—and the myriad genera available in commerce today are seldom offered by botanical names. Whatever they are called, they are invaluable to the arranger; buy them and use them fresh, then save them for dried displays. The huge, weird specimens like the one shown here demand a large scale and dramatic setting, but there are smaller varieties that go well with more familiar dried material. All are air-dried.

Rhus

R. typhina; Anacardiaceae

The staghorn sumac is a handsome American shrub or small tree of the same family as cashews and pistachios. The large, deep-red seed clusters have the same color and texture as the seats of old movie theaters. These clusters appear in July and persist on the shrubs until the following year, when new ones appear. They can be picked and air-dried any time in the late summer or autumn, but it is easier to wait for the foliage to drop naturally, after it has turned its brilliant autumnal scarlet.

Rosa

Rosa species, etc.; Rosaceae

Although the rose is not one of the easy flowers to dry, everyone seems to want to try. Some varieties, especially the pink sweetheart type, air-dry quite well; but silica gel is the best medium for most of the flowers. Roses can be dried at all stages of development, but full-blown specimens are likely to drop petals or to flop after drying. Be sure specimens are completely dry and in perfect condition. The colors may change somewhat—the very dark reds tend to become unattractive blackish shades—but some very subtle and interesting tones may result. Drying in silica will take three to eight days depending on the size of the flower. The species roses also produce wonderful hips for drying in late autumn. *Rosa multiflora* in particular makes great arching canes of clusters of bright red-orange berries. These will air-dry.

MC

108

Rudbeckia

R. hirta, R. triloba, R. fulgida;
Compositae

This cheerful American native, the black-eyed Susan, is a beloved sight along roadsides in July, but it is also universally known as a garden plant. The garden varieties, which are usually biennials or short-lived perennials, have much larger flowers with centers marked in shades of red, brown, and deep gold. These are among the easiest and most successful flowers for drying with sand or borax. The flowers wilt soon after they are picked, so it is best to condition them in warm water immediately. One species, *R. triloba,* has much smaller, more numerous flowers with sharp, dark centers. These air-dry; the black centers can also be used after the petals drop.

Rumex

R. acetosa; Polygonaceae

It is no surprise to find that these invasive weeds are relatives of the polygonum; they grow everywhere, are almost impossible to eradicate, and have the same redeeming feature of providing invaluable dried material. Dock is one of the staples of the everlasting collection. Picked at different stages throughout the summer, it will yield thick branches of reddish-green, red-gold brown, and finally deep brown. Some plants produce heavy club-like clusters, some thin spikes. Dock is practically dried when you pick it; just gather and store it until it is to be used.

AM

Rushes
Juncaceae

Although beginners tend to group all grass-like plants together, a little close-up examination of the rushes shows how different they are. Rushes have round, unjointed stems that are usually hollow or filled with a cottony pith; the flowers are arranged in a tuft at the top of the stem or emerge in a clump from one side. Although the flowers are not conspicuous, the whole stem makes an interesting dried specimen. Rushes are found in damp, open areas or around ponds and streams. They air-dry easily, but with the taller species—some can be ten feet tall—insert a wire up the stem to keep it straight.

AM

Salvia

S. superba, S. farinaceae, etc.; Labiatae

With over 700 species of salvia to choose from, it's hard to enumerate the best for drying. There are annuals, bienniels, and perennials in this genus. Almost all can be air-dried or dried in sand. The color range is enormous, from the fiery red of the familiar *S. splendens,* the medium blue of *S. farinaceae,* to the deep purple of *S. superba.* Even the culinary sage produces interesting silvery calyxes and foliage.

Sedges

Cyperaceae

"Sedges have edges and rushes are round" helps to distinguish between members of these grass-like families. The stems of sedges are triangular in cross section and unjointed, in contrast to rushes and grasses. Sedges are perennial plants of marshes and damp areas throughout North America and Britain. All air-dry easily. Picked at different stages, sedges will dry silvery grey, gold, or deep brown.

Sedum

Sedum species, etc.; Crassulaceae

The house leeks are "useful" rather than spectacular plants. They provide excellent filler material of subtly varied texture and tone. The varieties of *Sedum allbum* produce delicate, pinkish-white flowers that dry like a kind of statice or gypsophila; the mid-summer varieties with brilliant yellow flowers yield seed heads of rich brown later in the season. Most sedum are hardy perennials.

Silene

S. vulgaris, S. cucubalus, S. noctiflora; Caryophyllaceae

These campions are wild throughout Britain and North America. In most species, the petals emerge from a kind of inflated bladder, which dry well if picked when still green; later, after the flower has set seed, there are shiny brown seed capsules that can also be used. The silenes are related to the genus Lychnis, which produces similar drying material.

Solidago
S. canadensis, etc.; Compositae

North Americans are often puzzled or amused to find solidago in British or European garden catalogues; they are too accustomed to considering it a hay-fever-producing weed to appreciate its excellence as a cut flower and drying plant. (No, it does *not* produce hay fever; the culprit is ragweed, which blooms at the same time.) There is one European and British goldenrod, but it is not the best kind for drying. There are over 100 species in North America, offering a wide variety of flower formation—some narrow spikes, some dense plumes, some open, feathery clusters. All are useful. Air-dry them when one third of the flowers are open, the rest are bud—they will open while drying.

Remove the leaves and hang them to dry.

Spiraea

S. tomentosa, S. latifolia; Rosacea

Filipendula

F. ulmaria, F. vulgaris; Rosacea

All these species are referred to as meadow-sweet—another example of the confusion that results from the use of common names. These genera are related, since they are all in the rose family, but they resemble each other in very few other respects. The spiraea species are shrubby natives of North America and are related to the cultivated bridal wreath. They have narrow, upright spikes of pale- or deep-rose-pink flowers late in the summer. This is shown in the illustration. Filipendula is a wildflower in both Europe and the United States and also is widely grown as a garden plant. It is a tall perennial with open, airy clusters of tiny pink or white flowers; the stems are not woody and die back each winter. All these species can be air-dried; remove leaves and hang them.

Stachys
S. byzantina; Labiatae

Every part of this plant is covered with white, silky, woollike hair—hence the name woolly lamb's ears. It is grown in the herb garden for its pretty foliage, which makes a dense white mat. The flowering stalk is a fascinating addition to the collection of silver dried material—pick it before the flowers mature, and air-dry it. The stalks can be hung but some should be dried lying flat to preserve the curves. Turn them over every few days. Individual leaves can also be dried flat; they need no pressing.

AM

Tagetes

T. erecta, T. patula; Compositae

Marigolds are one of the essential plants of the annual summer garden. The tall varieties provide masses of yellow or orange cut flowers, and the smaller French type makes excellent edging and window-box plants. The enormous double orange are best for air-drying—they will shrink considerably but still provide a strong burst of color. Insert a wire up the hollow stem and through the flower head before hanging to make it easier to attach a stem after drying. The smaller varieties can be dried with silica or sand.

Tanacetum

T. vulgare; Compositae

Tansy brightens herb gardens and roadsides from the mid-summer to the autumn. Originally cultivated for culinary and medicinal uses, it is now a wild plant throughout Britain and North America. It resembles achillea in appearance and color, but the tansy clusters are formed by flat, button-like flowers with no edging of ray petals. Harvest it and let it air-dry at the peak of color, before it begins to turn brown.

Thalictrum

T. polyganum, T. dasycarpum, T. flavum; Ranunculaceae

Besides the lovely wild species found in Britain and North America, there are numerous species of thalictrum from Asia that have been developed as garden perennials. The flowers are airy, cloud-like clusters and can be air-dried just before the peak of bloom. Later, interesting clusters of seeds that can also be used are produced.

Thistle

Carduus, Carlina, Circium, Cnicus,
Onopordun species; Compositae

There are numerous species of thistles with yellow,
white, red, and purple flowers. All should be handled
with heavy gloves and care. Pick it before the head is
fully open—it will continue to open as it dries. If
picked later the blooms will shatter. Remove the
leaves and scrape any thorns from the lower part of
the stem.

Trifolium

T. agrarium; Leguminosae

The rabbit's-foot clover has silky, fluffy heads that
change in color from greenish to silvery pink as they
age—pick them at all stages of development. They
air-dry easily and make excellent material for small
arrangements and wreaths. The yellow hop-clover's
flowers don't retain their bright original color when
air-dried but fade to an attractive light brown. These
are found throughout Britain and North America.

Tulipa

Tulipa species, etc.; Liliaceae

Once you have developed your technique with silica gel, here is a flower to try. It is not an easy subject, and the results may be disappointing, but when successful the effort is worth it. There are so many colors, shapes, textures, and varieties of tulips that we can't begin to list them, but these wonderful bulbs are well-known to everyone and need little description. Pick just after the bud stage as they begin to open and show their real shape. When drying them, take care to retain the cup shape. They should dry in four to five days in silica. For those who prefer air-drying, the species tulips produce incredible pods in early summer.

AM

Typha

T. latifolia, T. angustifolia;
Typhaceae

Whether they are known as cattails or reed-maces, these large plants grown in swampy ground are common throughout Europe and North America. They are irresistible material for the flower arranger, but they must be handled properly. Often they are picked too late in the season; when brought inside they explode into cloudy masses of seeds and fluff. Pick cattails in July. It is best to get them while the male flowers—the golden tassels on the upper part of the stem—are still in bloom. Air-dry by standing them upright in a large container, or spread them flat. *T. angustifolia* has narrower leaves and heads and is better for smaller arrangements.

MC

Umbelliferae

So many good drying plants are found in this large family that it is only possible to name a few. Many herbs are umbelliferae—dill, parsley, lovage, caraway, coriander—as are some vegetables—carrots, celery, and fennel—and all have the same characteristic shape—the umbell. Their size varies enormously; huge heracleum for giant arrangements, and delicate seed heads of cumin for dainty miniatures. There are wild species throughout Europe and North America.

Verbascum

V. thapsus, V. blattaria, V. phoeniceum;
Scrophulariaceae

These tall, strong biennials are found in poor, rocky, waste places. The first year the plant makes a large rosette of silver, felt-like leaves—this entire cluster can be air-dried. The second year the flower spikes, sometimes six to eight feet tall, are produced and can also be air-dried. The more delicate moth mullein makes long stems of round seedpods.

Veronica

V. incana, V. spicata, V. longifolia, etc.;
Scrophulariaceae

Pretty veronicas include creepy, mat-like species as
well as tall clumps of spires. All have similar
flowers—long, narrow spikes of blue, white, or pink,
which open slowly over a long blooming period.
These can be dried in sand or silica when half are in
bloom and half are in bud. They can also be air-dried
at the same stage.

Zinnia

Z. elegans; Compositae

The zinnia brings vibrant colors to late-summer arrangements, and it can also be easily dried with sand
or silica. The flowers should be picked when fully
open, but before the centers have begun producing
pollen. The really enormous varieties may flop in high
humidity, but the medium and smaller kinds are
trouble-free. This is a somewhat tender annual; start
seeds indoors early for the longest period of bloom.

Chapter Six

Preliminaries and Afterthoughts

YOU HAVE BEEN HARVESTING FOR MONTHS and your flowers are now dried, but there are still a few essential steps before they are ready to be arranged and used. Some of these techniques—like storing, wiring, and attaching false stems—are somewhat tedious but nonetheless are essential to the arranger. Others are suggestions that might prove helpful with certain materials, or ideas to experiment with to obtain a specific effect. You will discover, now that you have mastered the basic drying methods, that there are ways of bending the rules to achieve the look you want; it is at this point that drying flowers becomes less of a series of techniques and more a creative process.

Wiring and Attaching Stems

WIRING IS DISCUSSED IN THE SECTION ON DRYING WITH desiccants, and is also mentioned in connection with air-drying strawflowers or gomphrena. To sum up: Flowers should be wired on short stubs (two to six inches in length) before drying. The wire is inserted into a short (one inch) section of natural stem left on the flower head and inserted partway into the head. Some plants, such as sedges and rushes and others with hollow stems, will benefit from having a wire inserted up into the natural stem before being air-dried. The best wire is green florist's wire, 20 to 24 gauge, which comes in a variety of lengths. A heavier weight (with a lower gauge number) may be necessary for very large specimens such as sunflowers and magnolias.

After drying, you will have a large collection of beautiful flower heads on very short wires. You can either add a natural stem of another kind of flower, or you can conceal the wire and add another to it with florists' wrapping tape. This tape, sometimes known as gutta percha, is a papery, slightly elastic substance that adheres tightly and smoothly to itself when stretched. It is available in a range of colors—the standard moss green and dark brown are the most useful for this work, although the pastels are helpful for wreaths and bridal bouquets. To wrap a wire stem, start the end of the tape at the head of the flower, above the point where the wire emerges. Turn the flower and move the tape down the stem, stretching the tape slightly as you go and smoothing it along the wire. If you wish to add a longer wire, overlap the new length with the original stem wire and wrap the two together. Several layers of wrapping can be applied, depending on the weight and size of the flower.

This kind of wiring is effective when used in a mass arrangement, where the stems will be concealed by filler and other flowers. For larger

Cover stem wire with florist's wrapping tape before arranging. Repair woody stems with a "splint" of wire and wrapping tape.

specimens, and in situations where the stem is exposed and a natural look is essential, a false stem must be used. In the course of your drying and arranging, extra stems are produced and should be saved from flowers that are used for very short filler or from flowers that dry badly and have to be discarded—some arrangers even harvest extra stems of certain plants. The best stems are strong, long and hollow, or with a soft pith. The skillful arranger will take great pains to find a stem that matches the scale and tone of the flower. Make a clean cut at the top of the stem and insert the stub wire of the flower head until both stem ends meet in a clean joint. A small drop of milk-based glue applied with a

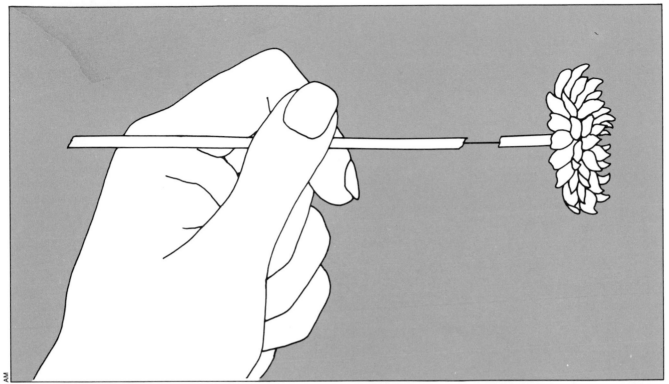

A false stem can easily be attached to a wired flower head. Insert the stub of wire into false stem until the two ends meet, then secure the joint with glue. Also use this method to lengthen natural stems or to repair broken ones.

toothpick will reinforce the joint. Some of the best stems to use are opium poppy, Siberian iris, yarrow, delphinium, and goldenrod.

The above method can be used to lengthen flowers dried on their natural stems—if the original stem will accept a wire after drying. If it will not, a "splint" can be made: Make a joint between the two stems by running two short lengths of wire on either side and wrapping the whole joint with tape. This should be done only if the joint will be concealed in the arrangement.

Smaller everlastings such as amobium, xeranthemum, or gomphrena are lovely for small arrangements but get lost in larger work. To display them to their advantage, gather them into loose clusters and wire them to a single stem. The same can be done with delicate grasses which would be lost by themselves but which create an effect in a bunch. Leaves which have been pressed separately or treated with glycerine can be assembled into clusters or palmate fans by wiring. Flowers can also be attached with fine wire or tape directly to large branches treated with glycerine.

Use the flexibility of wired flowers to avoid the straight, static lines characteristic of bad dried arrangements. Although it is a time-consuming and laborious process, wiring can be a tool for making your flowers look more alive.

127

A Few Words About Storage

IT WOULD BE WONDERFUL IF YOU COULD DRY FLOWERS then arrange them immediately. However, this is almost never the case. If you are drying with desiccants, much of your material is ready in mid-summer when you are busy arranging fresh flowers, so it must be stored until the fall. If you are air-drying and have lots of space, the material can be left hanging until you use it; but if your optimum drying space is limited, flowers will have to be removed to make way for late-flowering species.

Once material is air-dried it is fairly stable, but it should be preserved from mildew, insects, dust, dirt, and strong light. Large, long cardboard boxes will hold considerable quantities; there will be some breakage, but dried material is surprisingly tough. Wrap more delicate bunches in newspaper or tissue before placing them in the boxes. These boxes then can be stacked in a dry place.

Bunches can also be stored outside the drying room if they are protected with a wrapper of newspaper. Hang them almost anywhere you have space—once they are dry, they can be stored close together, and hanging will ensure that they keep their shape until used.

Flowers dried in sand, borax, or desiccants present the biggest storage problems. Material can be left in sand or borax until needed, but if you have to reuse the media or the boxes, storage is necessary. Flowers dried in silica must be removed as soon as they are dried.

Dried flowers must be carefully preserved from humidity until they are arranged, and every effort must be made to retain the perfect shape and color of

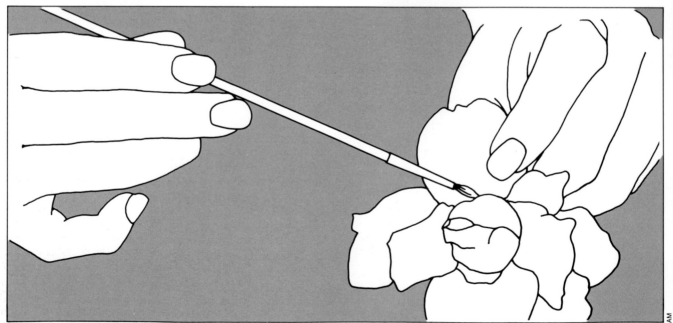

White glue is used to replace broken petals after drying—apply it sparingly with a toothpick or small brush.

the material. A large screen will accommodate many flowers facing upright with their wires hanging down. (This position is not good for cup-shaped flowers like lilies, tulips, or roses, which should be placed separately in paper cups to support their shape.) The screen must then be kept in a room with subdued light and humidity below 60 percent. If such a storeroom is not available, flowers must be packed in airtight tins. Make sure the flowers are secured so they will not move around and be damaged; they should not touch one another.

Pressed foliage can be left as it was dried—between layers of newspapers—until it is arranged. Foliage treated with glycerine can be wrapped in sheets of paper—this material is susceptible to mildew so don't use sheets of plastic. Large air-dried material such as pods and grasses can be stored in plastic bags.

Gluing

THE JUDICIOUS USE OF GLUE CAN SALVAGE BROKEN dried material and prevent breakage in advance, or to achieve certain effects. The most useful, all-around glue is a white, milk-based type that dries clear or slightly cloudy. This kind is completely harmless to people and plant material and can be diluted to any consistency.

Use glue to reinforce the petals of certain delicate floral varieties before you dry them—tulips, peonies, and some roses benefit from gluing. After drying, use glue to strengthen the stems of physalis at the point where the lanterns connect to the main stem. Bells of Ireland can be treated in a similar fashion. Petals broken in sand drying can be retrieved and discreetly repaired. After pressing autumn foliage, leaves can be reattached to their branches.

Apply glue in tiny quantities with a toothpick or a small brush. Be sure the glue is completely dry before placing the flowers or foliage in sand or silica, or before using them in an arrangement.

Varnishing

VARNISH OR SHELLAC HAS MANY USES IN ARRANGING. Dip feathery seed heads, like clematis, in varnish before the seeds mature—this will keep them shiny and intact. In some cases, applying varnish will keep seedpods from opening—epilobium pods can be treated in this way. However, it is better not to rely on varnish for that—milkweed pods cannot be stayed and should be used _after_ the seeds have ripened. Dipping in varnish may prevent cattails from shattering, but the only really foolproof method to prevent this is to pick them early in July.

Try varnishing any of the varieties of tree flowers or seeds—the drooping catkins of birch or alder, maple, or ironwood seeds. Varnish will enhance the colors of certain pods and add a nice sheen—the pods of baptisia, for example, become a much more dramatic black. Experiment carefully with various finishes—a high gloss is often too artificial looking and will inhibit your desired visual effect.

Artificial Coloring

IN GENERAL, COLORING IS NOT A RECOMMENDED technique. Too often the application of spray paint is used to disguise badly dried material. The emphasis in this book is on the natural beauty of dried material, not on the creation of something bizarre or peculiar. Still, it is possible to use certain sprays discreetly to highlight natural colors. Green foliage, in particular, can benefit from a little enhancement. There is also a clear floral paint spray which can be used like a light varnish (although it won't hold seed development like real shellac). It will give a slight sheen to flowers dried with desiccants. Special floral paints will not harm the material, but do experiment carefully to decide what you want. Be sure to remove all trace of sand, borax, or silica before you apply paint.

Chapter Seven

How to Use Everlastings

NOW IT'S TIME TO USE THIS GLORIOUS ARRAY of everlasting material you have assembled. Perhaps it seemed as if you would never get to this stage. Remember that much of the drying and preparation of material takes place a little at a time over a long period— it's not as time consuming as it might sound at first, especially as you develop your own short cuts. And here is the reward for all that careful preparation. What a wonderful luxury to arrange a wide selection of material. You have the harvest of four seasons spread before you.

The purpose of this book is not to give you step-by-step, arrange-by-number plans for standard arrangements—instead, it will give you the basic technical information necessary for arranging dried flowers and some suggestions for using them in less traditional ways. The photographs throughout the book show just some of the diversity of styles you can pursue. Be encouraged by them, not limited to them. Let your own selection of everlastings inspire a particular direction; your individual creativity will take it from there.

Fresh Versus Dried Arrangements

BEGIN BY THINKING ABOUT THE DIFFERENCES BETWEEN fresh and dried flower arrangements. Everlastings, by their nature, can never aspire to the nonchalant elegance and vitality that makes three live tulips in a glass vase so moving. Don't try to compete with that style—simply pursue others. It's an interesting paradox that, because of their static condition, everlastings require painstaking care to make them look natural. These arrangements, while they will not last forever, will be enjoyed for a longer time and should, therefore, they can be more highly detailed and have more complicated visual interest. The viewer should discover new things about them over time.

Information on Containers

MANY OF YOUR FAVORITE CONTAINERS FOR FRESH flowers can also be used for everlastings, with a few additions and exceptions. Glass vases, particularly clear glass, are generally *not* suitable—the dried stems and wires and the mechanics of assembly are not attractive when exposed. Also, glass will only accent the artificiality of the arrangement. This is the time to use all those nice pottery containers that don't hold water and those pretty baskets you could never find a liner for. Terra-cotta is an excellent foil for dried material. Remember that these containers will not be filled with water, so they must be weighted at the bottom with sand or stones in order to be stable—it is very easy to make them top heavy. An arrangement that keeps toppling over can be very annoying, and will soon look worse for wear. The container or arrangement can also be affixed to a heavy base.

Notes on Construction

THE HEAVY PRUNING SHEARS YOU HAVE BEEN USING ALL along for gardening and harvesting are also invaluable for construction. A wire cutter or tin snip will be necessary for wire stems and for cutting chicken wire. Keep various weights of florist wire on hand for stem repairs. Rolls of green or brown florists' wrapping tape will be needed, as will florists' dark green adhesive tape, which is very strong and especially formulated to hold to slippery metal, china, or pottery surfaces. A spool of very fine wire—silver or brass—is useful. Long tweezers are handy for inserting delicate material. White, milk-based glue and a small brush are necessary for final touchups and petal repairs.

Knowing in advance where the final arrangement will be displayed will influence your choice of container, the overall size of the arrangement, and the appropriate color range and style. It is important to know if the arrangement will be seen from all angles, or if it is to be one-sided (in a niche or against a wall). As a general indication of proportion, in most finished products the container is one-third, and the flowers two-thirds the height of the whole—this proportion can be varied somewhat with long, low pieces.

Depending on the weight and size of the container, fill the bottom few inches with sand or gravel. Then insert Styrofoam or the grey-green florists' foam used for the construction of fresh arrangements. Special brown foam is made for dried flowers; it is stiffer and holds large stems better than the green absorbent variety. The foam should stick up an inch or two above the top of the container.

Arrangements of very large materials work best with chicken wire as a base. The wire can be used either on top of the foam to reinforce it or alone, crumpled up, in the container. Chicken wire should also stick up from the top of the vase. Foam or wire

ROBERT GRAY

A classic arrangement of silica-dried flowers and glycerine-treated leaves complements a gracious setting.

Several varieties of foliage provide the roughly triangular background form for this traditional arrangement.

Sprays of artemesia, goldenrod, and delphinium make a more graceful outline and offer contrast in color and texture.

can be tightly wedged in a tall, narrow vase. For baskets or pots with wide, open tops, the foam or wire should be secured tightly to the sides with florists' adhesive tape.

Since everlastings need no water, they can also be arranged using a non-traditional container. A block of foam can be attached directly to a base—a branch of driftwood, for example—and the arrangement made on it. After completion any visible parts of the construction can be covered with moss, stones, or filler.

It is important not to hurry when arranging everlastings. Take time to study the material and decide how to use it. All stiff up-and-down lines

should be avoided; almost all stems should be inserted at a slight angle, so that the overall effect is that the flowers radiate—almost explode—from the center. Find subtle curves in the material and use them to advantage. Make sure flowers and leaves curve down and around the sides and front of the container. Notice how a specific plant grows and you will get hints about how to display it most beautifully.

A traditional, upright, one-sided arrangement using glycerine-treated foliage and flowers dried in desiccant most resembles a traditional fresh flower arrangement in its design and construction. The branches of the leaves are inserted first to form the

ROBERT GRAY

Silica-dried zinnias, dahlias, tulips—all harvested from the summer garden—complete this year-round bouquet.

This free-form, sculptural arrangement is a dramatic feature in a modern office environment.
All material is air-dried and needs little maintenance.

background and to establish the overall shape and size. Contrasting material—this can be air-dried filler material—is then inserted to fill in the shape and to provide more texture. *Chrysanthemum parthenium,* delphinium, celosia, or contrasting leafy material like artemesia can be used as filler. Then add the central focal material—silica-dried dahlias and zinnias, for example.

Another traditional style, which could be called the Colonial American style, uses no green foliage at all. This is an informal mixture (usually in baskets or pots) of grasses, pods, and air-dried material intended to resemble the fields in late summer or fall—this type of arrangement usually has no definite focal point. The informal look of this kind of arrangement is misleading; painstaking care is necessary to achieve its nonchalance. An overall cover of filler—grasses, mustards, small pieces of dock—is first spread across the entire open surface of the container. This filler conceals the foam and makes a variegated, textured base for the arrangement. Gradually build up with larger and longer pieces—work all around the basket and keep turning it to ensure that the shape is uniform all around. Here, too, all stems should emerge from the center at an angle, and without crisscrossing. Groom your material as you work; trim broken stems and eliminate discolored flowers or leaves. Gradually add color and more flowing material—solidago, tanacetum, yarrow, rose hips, bittersweet—as the arrangement fills up. For the final touch, add a few rudbeckia dried in borax and air-dried wild carrot.

The styles described above are probably the most familiar kinds of everlasting arrangements. They are different in their construction, in the material they use, and in the overall effect they create. There are many, many styles in between, depending on your individual setting, containers, and selection of everlastings.

There is also a very modern style of dried arrangement that is less directly related to fresh-flower styles. This boldly uses the most dramatic dried material—large branches, fantastic pods, strange exotics like protea. These can create wonderful uncompromising and aggressive sculptured effects. In spite of the apparent free form of this style, however, it is just as carefully constructed as a period arrangement for a Regency drawing room. The energy and seeming freedom of the material is the result of great preparation and thought, as well as good design sense.

It's not difficult to find different examples of arrangements to imitate, once you become adept at handling dried material. But imitation should not be your only goal. Once you have spent several seasons observing flowers, growing them, and gathering them in the wild, you will have learned almost unconsciously a great deal about the complicated interplay of plants in the environment. Create arrangements that reflect this interest and knowledge—they will do greater justice to your material and your own originality.

Suggestions for Wreaths

THERE ARE COUNTLESS OTHER DECORATIVE WAYS everlastings can be used. At present, one of the most popular is the creation of wreaths of dried flowers. This is a wonderful way to display everlastings, since wreaths don't require table space or a stand the way an arrangement does.

You can buy ready-made straw bases for wreaths, but often they are too tightly woven to allow the addition of flowers, and it's not difficult to make your own base.

Select a bowl, pot, or container the same size as the finished wreath you want—the inside of the bowl will be the outside circumference of the wreath. Begin placing straw, grasses, or light twiggy material in a circle inside the bowl. It is easiest to work continually in one direction. Bend the material along the sides of the bowl, keeping the

This lush wreath combines warm colors and rich textures.

center open. Continue until the desired thickness is obtained—this will vary with the overall size of the wreath, but be sure it is solid and firm.

Gently lift one section away from the side of the bowl. Wrap the wreath with thread, string, or fine wire and tie it, anchoring it to the wreath. Then continue gently lifting the rest of the wreath, winding with the string as you go. The circles of string don't have to be very close together the first time around—after you have encircled the entire wreath once, go back around, smoothing loose ends, and firming places where necessary. Tie string securely. Now go back and clip off any remaining twig ends. With a wire or thread, attach a hanger on the back. For very large-sized wreaths, you can purchase metal frames from a florist supply house. They can be covered with layers of chicken wire, and then covered with sheets of moss. A natural, open base can be made of grape vines.

The fun, of course, is in deciding how to decorate your wreath—the possibilities are limited only by your time and supply of material. Stems should be inserted firmly into the base or secured under the wrapping wire or thread. Extremely fragile material should not be used on outdoor wreaths or those which will hang on interior doors that are frequently opened or slammed. Remember, *all* dried material will eventually fade in strong sunlight.

© RICHARD S. DUNCAN 1984

A lively swirl of air-dried grasses displays many subtle shades.

Wreaths like the ones shown here are clearly not limited to any particular season, but everlastings make lovely holiday displays. Garlands or swags can be made for autumnal, harvest decorations on stairways or mantles. Combine interesting pods with fruit and nuts for a Della Robbia effect.

At Christmastime, everlastings are a wonderful addition to evergreen wreaths and garlands. This is a good time to use old pods or seed heads which, although faded, are still in good condition. A spray of gold or silver paint will give this material new life—use them with live flowers in holiday centerpieces and other arrangements.

Beautiful and unexpected holiday decorations can be made by combining eucalyptus and heather with evergreens, white branches, and silver pods and cones. Some designers decorate entire Christmas trees with gypsophila or limonium—in fact, miniature tabletop trees can be constructed of these materials on a chicken-wire base covered with moss.

By now many possibilities of everlastings are probably beginning to occur to you, and it's time to take off on your own. Experiment and make mistakes—it doesn't matter, since you can easily take everything apart and start over. At worst, you may have to put on some new stems. Enjoy the everlastings you have harvested; enjoy the many ways they can be used. And enjoy yourself!

Sources

ONE APPEALING ASPECT OF WORKING WITH DRIED flowers is that it requires little in the way of expensive or difficult-to-find equipment and supplies. Since this book is intended for readers in several different countries, it is not possible in most cases to recommend specific brands or supply sources, but we can make general suggestions about where to look for the materials you may need.

The most important piece of equipment for anyone working with flowers, fresh or dried, is a good pruning shears, or secateurs. The swiss brand, Felco, is one of the best and is widely available. When buying any brand, it is important to be sure to get the best quality you can find, regardless of cost. Hardware stores and garden centers usually carry a good selection.

Most of the other supplies necessary can be purchased at a good garden center. They often carry some flower-arranging tools (most of which you don't need), as well as florist wire and tape. You may find that they sell green florist foam, such as Oasis® and Quickee, and/or regular Styrofoam. These can be used dry for everlastings, but the best is Sahara™, a brown foam especially designed for dried flowers.

If you belong to a garden club, you can order any of these supplies wholesale, which is the easiest way to get them. Otherwise, look in hobby shops or arts and crafts centers. Occasionally, a variety store like Woolworth's will carry these things. Botanical gardens or horticultural societies sometimes have shops that carry florist's supplies; if not, it's possible they can recommend a place which does. If you have a good local florist, you can probably get him to sell you what you need.

Look for silica gel, which is not very easy to find, in any of the above places. Or, mail-order sources are often advertised in garden magazines or journals and some seed and bulb catalogues offer their own brands. One good source in America is Roberta Moffitt, P.O. Box 3597, Wilmington, DE, 19807. She makes her own brand, Petalast, and has a catalogue of other supplies.

Borax and cornmeal are both available at the supermarket and are inexpensive. Sand can be purchased from a hardware store or building-supply center; be sure it is fine grain and as clean as possible.

The best type of glue to use is a white, milk-based variety like Elmer's or Sobo, sold in supermarkets and stationery stores. Some arrangers prefer the clear glue used for model airplanes and other hobbies, but the fumes are toxic or at least allergenic. It is not necessary to use a very strong super-glue for this kind of work.

Glycerine is available at a pharmacy. But, if you are going to do this kind of drying, try to order it wholesale from a drug-supply house, since you will need a lot and it is expensive.

Other supplies mentioned in the book can be found in hardware stores: chicken wire, varnish or shellac, fine wire, hooks, string, etc. But, in any event, flower arrangers are usually very inventive and can find materials that can be effectively substituted for anything they can't find.

MEASURE EQUIVALENTS		
	American Units	**Metric Units**
LINEAR MEASURE	1 inch	25.4 millimeters 2.54 centimeters
	1 foot	30.48 centimeters 3.048 decimeters 0.3048 meter
	1 yard	0.9144 meter
LIQUID MEASURE	1 fluid ounce	29.573 milliliters
	1 quart	9.4635 deciliters 0.94365 liter
	1 gallon	3.7854 liters
DRY MEASURE	1 quart	1.1012 liters

Index